Scan to access
this book's resources

About the author

With over 33 years of experience, Chris Torres is a seasoned entrepreneur and marketing expert. His journey began at 16, diving into the world of work as an illustrator for children's educational books. From there, he taught himself graphic design, web design, and marketing, founding Senshi Digital 13 years later.

Recognising a passion for tourism marketing, Chris transformed Senshi into the Tourism Marketing Agency (TMA), catering to clients globally. His expertise has earned TMA prestigious awards and partnerships with industry leaders like Gray Line. Chris also works as a marketing coach, sharing his wealth of knowledge with aspiring entrepreneurs.

In addition to his coaching endeavours, Chris is also part-owner of Tourpreneur, a vibrant community of over 14,000 tour operators (at time of writing). Through Tourpreneur he continues to support and empower professionals in the tours and activities sector, fostering collaboration and growth within the industry.

First published, 2024
by The Marketing Coach, Chris Torres
Copyright © 2024 by Chris Torres

Although every precaution has been taken to verify the accuracy of the information contained herein, the author and publisher assume no responsibility for any errors or omissions. No liability is assumed for damages that may result from the use of information contained within.

Cover Design: Chris Torres
Interior Design: Chris Torres
Publisher: The Marketing Coach, Chris Torres

ISBN: 9781916147324

First Edition

Contents

Praise

"Required reading for tour operators wishing to take more responsibility for marketing and distribution rather than leaving it to their reseller channel. That should be all operators!!" **Rod Cuthbert, Founder for Viator**

"Chris Torres has the ability to execute marketing strategies that are unlike anything I've seen in the tour & activity industry. He and his team don't just hit the bullseye, they blow it to pieces... again and again." **Matthew Newton, Leatherback Travel & Former Director of Marketing at PeekPro**

"This isn't some 'get rich quick' look at the tour and activities market. Chris obviously knows his stuff and this shines through in this book. I have it on Kindle and then bought a paper copy so that I could bend pages/highlight and scribble notes on it. Yes, it's one of those books! I dare not recommend it to anyone from my city... because I'd rather my competition didn't buy it!" **R. F. Howie**

"So glad I bought this book. I started my wine tour business last year, and thought I was out of ideas on how I could improve my business, but thought 'what's to lose?' from buying this book. Since most people find me online, my website is my biggest marketing tool. Chris gets this, so focuses on the online experience, teaching us how to use all of the Google tools for research and better ranking, Trip Advisor, YouTube, insight into all the top social media platforms, and lots of other digital tools. This is literally a 'how to' for setting these tools up, so that I don't need to spend hours online trying to figure out how to do it myself. Not only does he tell me how to do it, but gives me ideas on WHAT to do. I now have a ton more ideas on how to increase sales, make more money, and do things more efficiently. Buy this book!" **Ali**

"Chris Torres is simply a top chap offering lots of useful free advice which is priceless. His input and free information has been very helpful to me and many more in the tour business. All in all, one of the leading brains in the digital marketing world of the tour business and one you should connect with today." **Chris Wilson, Typically Swiss Tours**

"Chris lives and breathes the tours and activities sector. As a newcomer to the adventure tours market, I have found the resources and learning material a great boost to my learning and growing — including the book 'How to Turn Your Online Lookers into Bookers'. Not only the nuts and bolts, but the creation of a fantastic support network and group of like minded souls within the social media structure to keep the growth and development of this industry thriving and surviving. Much appreciated." **Chris Wain, Tour Guide for Diageo**

"Chris' book was packed full of GREAT information! We used this time to revamp our webpage and marketing platforms and it has really made a difference! Our online bookings keep rolling in and it has helped our small paddle company so much! Thank you for the incredible service you are providing operators around the world!" **Katrina, Adventure Outdoor Paddle**

"This is a no-nonsense practical read. I wasn't a 'client' as such but when Covid-19 hit Chris offered one hour online consultations.

As a small operator the opportunity to bounce ideas off someone external to my business was invaluable. We don't have a huge marketing / consultant budget so to be able to connect on this basis was very helpful. I am based in Australia, Chris in Scotland but the challenges are the same world-wide. I intend to continue engaging with Chris on an ad-hoc basis and would highly recommend his services." **Lee-Anne Harris, Walk Brisbane**

"Chris always provides practical and realistic actions for all kinds of tour operators. His great approach stems from his top notch professionalism and care for his customers and the whole industry! Well done Chris and to everyone on the team! Keep it up!" **Daphne Tsevreni, Clio Muse**

"I have been an activity operator for almost 20 years and I decided to buy a copy of Turning lookers into Bookers and I can't be more happy about the decision. The quality and extent of all the book exceed my initial expectations. Many thanks for sharing all this knowledge with the tours and activity community!" **José Daniel Sanz, EloFLY**

"This is a book of pure gold! I wish I had found it before I set up my company, but I'm still learning SO MUCH! I'm taking it page by page, and implementing everything. No matter how established your company is, read this book!" **Sara Freeland**

"Chris is the irst person I call upon with any tour marketing challenges. This book is a must read." **Alex Bainbridge, CEO of Autoura & Former CEO & founder of TourCMS**

"I am a huge admirer of Chris Torres. The man gives away so much knowledge around increasing revenue for free... If I watched one of his videos I could have saved myself $400!" **Shane Whaley, Head of Community at Fareharbor**

"Amazing book! As a small tour company that is just in the beginning of its road to success. We found this book a major guide on our path! Advice to other readers: don't miss even a single letter from this book!" **Akmal Said**

"Everything I've read from Chris is thought-provoking. All of it. He gives real insight and makes me a better manager by having to ask myself a lot of questions about my business. Thanks Chris for your time and advice." **Inma Bezunartea, Rioja Wine Trips**

My initial experience with digital marketing did not go well. I am so glad I widened my search and went with what must be the best travel marketing company on Earth! I know we are only at the beginning of the marketing journey, but the journey to date has been incredible." **Damien Stewart, Poland at War Tours**

"Chris is an amazing resource. As a very small tour company, I was amazed by his honesty, openness, and immediate support of my requests. This is a gem of a human... a rare find. " **Justin Legge, Tour Director at Redwood Adventures and Elk Meadow Cabins**

"We have been with the Tourism Marketing Agency for a number of years and they have been excellent for our growth and results. Chris and his team deliver on every occasion, are always there when you need them and can help grow your business to the next level. Would highly recommend them." **Reinier Van der Maat, Overland Ireland**

"I just want to say thank you to the whole team at Tourism Marketing Agency for the huge milestone of launching my new brand and website, and thereby making a dream come true for me. I couldn't have made it this far without your help. Outstanding work and highly recommended." **Carol El Hawary, Helwa Tours and Mr & Mrs Egypt**

"Chris and his team have been instrumental in helping us grow the Gray Line Iceland brand. The extra bookings and revenue we have received from their marketing efforts have been nothing short of remarkable." **Hrafnkell Konráðsson, Former E-commerce Manager at Gray Line Iceland**

"Chris and his team were instrumental in our food tour company tripling our sales from last year. We also increased our direct sales by 463%! Our rebrand they directed us through was a tremendous improvement from our old stuff. They consistently go above and beyond and beat expectations. Not only that, they are also extremely personable and a joy to work with. I highly recommend their team." **Dan Morris, Alaskan Sights and Bites**

"Chris and his team have given invaluable advice and guidance to help my small tourism business. He provides a lot of free resources such as his book and podcasts that we have found so helpful and uplifting during the pandemic. Thank you so much." **Rebecca**

" I came to know about Chris through a webinar which introduced Facebook marketing techniques for tours and activities. I downloaded his book "Turn Lookers into Bookers" and subscribed to his newsletters.

His content and shared knowledge (free) is highly useful and relevant to me in Sydney and I share his principles with my advisory clients in culinary tourism. I would love to bring Chris to Australia for a speaking series. His outside-the-box-push-the-envelope thinking and inspiration is just what Australia needs in the 'new normal' for tourism." **Viktoria Darabi, Savvy & Successful**

"Top-notch resources and emails that are always full of great ideas. Chris's book, Lookers into Bookers is the bible for tourism operators - I would be lost without it." **Justin S**

Preface

Why this book is for you

Foreword by Brian Cain

"Implementing the information in Chris' book, and the notes from our call, helped my business grow by almost 400%. "

Being a tour operator isn't easy; we own, manage, guide, schedule, develop, sell, and market. That's a lot of hats for one person, so feeling overwhelmed is likely, and I'll be the first to admit, I've been there. If you're reading this foreword, I believe you've likely been there, too. I'm Brian Cain, owner of Crawl USA, and I was once sitting in a similar place to you today, searching for the coveted secret sauce in tourism marketing.

I'd spent countless hours watching generic marketing videos on YouTube, buying Russell Brunson books on Amazon, but none seemed to apply directly to my tour business. Then I discovered the Tourprenuer Facebook Group: a community of tour operators from all over the world sharing information on their experiences within the industry. That's where I found Chris Torres.

Chris was an active community member, constantly sharing knowledge in an easy-to-understand fashion while never attempting to self-promote; he genuinely wanted to help people.

After a few months of re-reading any comment by Chris, I found out about his podcast, The Digital Tourism Show, and then his book, How To Turn Your Online Lookers into Bookers (although I didn't buy it). I wanted the opportunity to have a conversation with

Brian & Chris at Arival San Diego, 2022

Chris, so I went out on a limb and messaged him, asking if he'd be available for that, and, fortunately for me, he obliged. Before this video call, I had no expectation or idea of how impactful it would be for my business.

On that call, Chris shared information that most marketing agency owners would likely keep in their back pocket in hopes that I may hire their company's services. I frantically wrote down notes and drew a diagram on a small dry-erase board which would eventually become a marketing blueprint for my business, Crawl New Orleans.

Now, full disclosure here, I didn't end up hiring Chris or TMA.

We were only a few short months into the pandemic, and with such an uncertain future in tourism, I couldn't move forward, and Chris was gracious and understanding. In a follow-up e-mail, Chris included a link to download a free digital copy of How To Turn Online Lookers into Bookers, and at this point, I've spent dozens of hours reading and revisiting it.

Implementing the information in Chris' book and the notes from our call helped my business grow by almost 400%.

I finally had the privilege of properly meeting Chris at an Arival event in San Diego. I thanked him and explained his knowledge and generosity in sharing had helped my business grow exponentially. After telling him my story and graciously thanking him repeatedly, he asked if I'd be interested in telling all of you about my experience.

While I can't promise a tourism marketing secret sauce exists, I can attest that we're most likely to find it in the pages of this book and following any tourism marketing advice from Chris Torres.

Brian Cain
Crawl Entertainment

Introduction by Peter Syme

The tours, activities and experiences marketplace is, without doubt, the best part of the travel industry. Those that operate in it are privileged to go to work each day with the sole overriding objective of making people smile and have fun.

The vast majority of the industry is made up of small operators who are obsessed with their product, service and making their guests happy. To be able to do this, they have to attract guests to their business, and that involves marketing. With all the advances in this digital age — with new technology and communication channels, you would think that it has become more straightforward. The reality is that it has become more difficult.

A small operator now has to be a small media business with an in-depth understanding of a wide range of marketing and distribution methods. Including Google, SEO, SEM, PPC, Local. Social media marketing via networks such as Facebook, Instagram, Twitter, Linkedin, Youtube. Communication channels that now include, phone, email, messaging apps, artificial intelligent bots. Distribution via direct and indirect use of global scale OTA partners which involves using reservation system technology with API connections.

Understanding the above language spaghetti is hard enough, never mind implementing it, and it was not why we operators got into this industry.

I have always taken the view that the customer experience begins before they meet the operator. The operator will deliver the best experience if they have had a direct relationship with the customer beforehand.

Your website is your window to the world, and it is here that you want to spend the most time and effort making sure it is designed and structured in a way that is mobile responsive. If it is suitable for your business, taking online bookings is critical. To be found online, your site needs time and effort, and money has to be invested in SEO. I am personally still getting returns each year from SEO work we did over a decade ago. If you are in a niche, and many of us are, this is where your focus should be.

Once your website is the very best it can be and you are ranking well in search results, it is impossible not to pay serious attention to social media. And, in my opinion, Facebook is a hugely underused channel for small operators. You have to plan on continuous work producing content, and it never ends, but it does deliver. We have personally filled multi-day high priced expeditions exclusively from Facebook and driven thousands of day customers via the platform.

The sorry news, folks, is that you will have to start to understand all of this stuff if your business is going to grow and thrive. The good news is that the industry is full of knowledgeable people and companies who have been through the pain and are willing to help. Chris is one of these people and has condensed thousands of hours of knowledge and skill from working with hundreds of operators across the world into this one book which is targeted

100% at helping small operators improve their businesses.

I wish I had this book 20 years ago. It could have saved me years of work and lots of failed marketing investments. I strongly recommend you read it. More importantly, I strongly suggest that you start to implement what it says and do not just put it on the shelf; it should be on your desk as a constant reference.

Pete Syme
Tourpreneur

Chris, Mitch Bach and Pete 'Yoda' Syme about to run one of our Tourpreneur Huddles - a business growth retreat for tour operators.

My own customer journey

If you read my last book, you can skip this section if you wish. If you did not, then I urge you to continue as it highlights an effective customer purchase journey....

This story is real and is a prime example of why this book matters to every tour and activity business.

During my early school years, my fascination with Japan began. Credit goes to my father for this. One assignment asked us to design a mood board about a historical event. While many chose mainstream topics, like the world wars or ancient Egypt, I wanted something unique.

One evening, I delved into my father's book collection (this was a time before the age of Google). My father, an avid reader, regularly received a collection of books from Reader's Digest. Among them, "The Ancient History of Japan" piqued my interest. Its cover, adorned with a Samurai warrior, was unlike anything I'd seen before. The magnificence of that warrior ignited my passion for everything Japanese.

Fast forward a couple of decades, my wife and I were at a crossroads, planning a momentous trip before we embarked on our journey into parenthood. The contenders? Canada and Japan. Needless to say, Japan stole the show, and we embarked on planning our unforgettable two-week adventure.

Our dream was to traverse Japan, soaking in its beauty. A brief online search led us to a company that stood out, all thanks to their compelling content.

Their video content, often helmed by their enthusiastic tour guides, was the selling point. One guide, Tyler Palmer, played a pivotal role in painting a vivid picture of the wonders awaiting us in Japan. His description of the sunrise atop Mt. Fuji, though initially daunting, became a bucket list item for us. Despite our hesitations about the climb, the company assured us of its feasibility, barring altitude sickness concerns. This led us to extend our trip to almost a month, making room for more such experiences.

Upon landing at Narita Airport, to our delight, Tyler Palmer greeted us. Having seen his videos, this felt like reuniting with a long-lost friend. It set the stage for an unparalleled Japanese experience.

From bustling cities to serene towns, from friendly locals to delectable cuisine, our Japanese experience was nothing short of magical. And, the crowning moment? Reaching Mt. Fuji's summit, a memory etched in our hearts forever.

Fast forward to today, nearly a decade later, we are still friends with Tyler and keep in communication through Facebook. He now also has a not so young family.

The crux of sharing this journey is to highlight the lasting impact of authentic marketing. One exemplary video led us to contact the company, extend our trip, refer countless others, and foster lasting relationships. This is the sheer power of genuine storytelling

We made it to the top of Mt. Fuji!

Sunrise at the top of Mt Fuji. A sight I will never forget.

coupled with strategic marketing. This is how powerful marketing can be.

With this book, my aim is to provide you with the tools and know-how to build your own 'tribe' of loyal customers and brand advocates, promoting your business in the right way. I will not only provide practical advice, but worksheets and videos, to assist you along the way.

I've tried to make this book an interesting read from cover to cover, but I know not everyone reads that way. This is also why the book is broken down into sections, allowing you to easily navigate to an area you're particularly interested in.

I do however urge you to read this book from cover to cover as, even if you know how to manage one aspect of digital marketing, I may be able to provide some new insight that helps you improve your processes in some way.

Let your journey begin...

Who is this book for?

This book is for any tour operator, tourism or hospitality business, marketing agency, or team looking to better understand the most effective way to market a travel related business.

Although the focus of the strategy in this book is for a multi-day tour operator, the premise and structure of the strategy is the same approach I take for any experience-based business. Of course, content and target demographics may change, but how you talk, engage, and inspire your target audience, — the storytelling element — will always remain the same.

This book is for anyone looking to get a better handle on how the many different individual elements of marketing fit together to become one, cohesive strategy that guides the consumer along the purchase journey and beyond — which is a long-winded way of saying that it will help you turn lookers into bookers.

Why write another book?

Honestly, I never thought I would ever write one book, let alone a follow up.

There was always that doubt in my mind when writing How To Turn Your Online Lookers Into Bookers that I was wasting my time. Who in their right mind would read a book written by me?

Well, it seems I was wrong, and not only that, there was a huge appetite in tour and experience operators to learn the 'basics' of marketing a tourism business and to learn some of the more advanced tactics my marketing agency deploys.

What really pushed me to write a follow up was when I spoke to Brian Cain of Crawl USA at an Arival event in San Diego. Brian is not a client of mine or the Tourism Marketing Agency (TMA) but he took the time to speak to me about how my book, podcasts, and videos have helped him shape his business. It was humbling that I'd played a small part in helping him. And Brian was not the only person at that event who approached me to say that my book had helped.

When writing the original book, I saw there was a gap in marketing knowledge for a lot of operators I speak to on a regular basis. Helping Brian and others like him has made writing my first book completely worthwhile.

Five years on, at time of writing, it has been purchased and downloaded over 20,000 times and helped countless others grasp what it takes to market their business to drive direct bookings.

Did I get rich writing that book? Of course not. In fact I lost money as the print and global shipping costs for the initial run of a 400 page book meant I spent more than I made, but I became rich in other ways as it grew the awareness of myself and my agency, TMA. More importantly, I helped many others in the tourism industry at a time when we all needed help.

When I started writing Lookers into Bookers: The Tourism Marketing Blueprint, I did not want to just rehash what I did before; I wanted it to expand on what I wrote, focusing more on a full strategy of a single operator rather than individual aspects or how to set up various platforms... all of that is already covered in my first book.

What I hope you will see in this book is a full, cohesive strategy from the birth of a new brand to the initial 6-month marketing strategy we created for one of my clients while also highlighting the real results of our efforts — for better or worse.

You will see each aspect we create as well as understand why we took specific directions I will try my best to explain as much detail as possible along the way so that you can get a deeper understanding of what it takes to drive direct bookings and have a sense of the amount of work a proper brand and marketing strategy should involve. If your own marketing teams or agencies are not doing half of what I suggest here, then you have some questions to ask.

Now, this does depend on your marketing budget with your agency. Please do not expect to pay a couple of hundred dollars, pounds or euros a month for everything I mention in this book. That will not happen!

Remember what I said in How To Turn Your Online Lookers Into Bookers. You must become a media company to compete in today's market. This has not changed; if anything, what the pandemic period taught us, it is even more important.

Real strategy. Real operator.

Everything you will see in this book is 100% the strategy we took for Egyptian-based operator Sina Tours. No filter. No bullshit. Just the facts.

In this book, I will cover the exact approach we took to help Sina Tours grow their leads, bookings and, ultimately, their business. It is important to understand not only the processes we take, but the sales process Sina Tours also takes as this plays a huge role in how successful a strategy will be.

The reason I mention this is because I have seen marketing campaigns that are extremely successful at generating new leads yet some operators become overwhelmed quickly as they don't have the resources to manage the influx of leads and bookings. Marketing is absolutely vital, but it is just as important to make sure your business has the right tools and people in place to sell and manage the increase in customer interest that comes with effective marketing practices.

I talk from experience. I remember almost 15 years ago when my agency helped one company and we generated over 800 qualified leads in the space of one month. I then got a call from the owner that he was disappointed that he got no leads from the campaign... Understandably, this started to ring alarm bells.

I went to his office, sat down and showed him all the leads stored in the back end of his website (which we showed his sales team how to access). To say he was shocked was an understatement. He had a full team of around ten sales executives and not one single lead was contacted.

To understand the full magnitude of this monumental screw-up, consider that all these leads added up to a potential sales value of over £2,400,000 GBP. Even if they only closed 1%, that would have generated £24,000 in sales — bear in mind that the industry standard for multi-day is a close rate of around 30%.

So, making sure you have a process in place to manage bookings and sales enquiries is absolutely vital before you spend a penny on marketing!*

*Test and measure, wins and losses are all part of marketing. It is how you learn what is working well or not. With this book, you will see all sides.

Understanding the customer journey

Understanding the customer journey is paramount. Every potential traveller embarks on a unique voyage from the initial spark of inspiration to the ultimate sharing of their experiences.

Picture the journey like a road trip with several exciting stops along the way: dreaming, planning, booking, experiencing, and sharing. Oh, and don't forget the occasional detour that many forget about, called cancellation. Below is an explanation of each stage...

Dreaming

The journey begins with the dreaming stage, where customers explore destination options with boundless curiosity and no concrete plans. This is the time for inspiration, for capturing imaginations and planting the seeds of wanderlust. As a tour operator, we must identify the platforms and content that inspire this exploration, positioning your destinations as irresistible possibilities.

Your aim is not to sell but to captivate, igniting a sense of wonder and excitement that centres on your destination. You must craft compelling narratives and immersive content that beckons travellers to envision themselves exploring your landscapes, indulging in your culture, and savouring your experiences. By painting vivid pictures and showcasing the allure of your destination, you plant the seeds of desire, ensuring that your brand remains at the forefront of their travel fantasies.

The approach you take during the dreaming stage will vary depending on whether you're promoting a day tour or a multi-day tour. Regardless of the type, this is where content that evokes emotion and inspiration plays a crucial role.

For multi-day tours, given the extended decision-making process, your content should be designed to captivate and draw attention to your destination. Potential customers might not have considered your location before, so this is your opportunity to showcase destination guides, engaging blogs, captivating videos, or downloadable PDF lead magnets on your website.

At this early stage, I recommend leveraging Meta Advertising (Facebook and Instagram) to target your ideal customer profile. Once they engage with your content—whether by reading or downloading—you can retarget them with additional ads that continue to inspire and gently guide them towards the planning stage. Regular, motivational automated emails can also be highly effective in maintaining their interest.

For day tours, the dreaming stage tends to be much shorter, as most customers are making their purchases in-destination. Although not always the case, this is typically true for many day tour operators.

For day tours, your content should aim to spark a sense of immediate need or desire rather than focusing solely on the destination. For instance, if you operate a food tour company, you might run ads in your destination with a question like, "Craving delicious local food and culture?" Direct them to an article highlighting some of the incredible places featured on your tour (ensure it goes beyond just replicating your tour description), with a compelling call to action to book their experience.

Even for day tours, you can attract potential customers before they arrive by using what I call a pre-ad or pre-content strategy. Target the areas where your customers predominantly come from with videos and shorts posted on social media platforms. Rather than promoting your business directly, focus on a particular aspect of your tour or destination.

A fantastic example of this is Justin Buzzi's video from Get Up and Go Kayaking, showcasing bioluminescent waters in Florida (https://www.youtube.com/watch?v=TFdZIEQVFBk). His video went viral, inspiring viewers to consider visiting Florida, even if they hadn't previously thought of it. The goal here is not to sell but to tap into the emotional appeal of the destination.

Planning

As travellers transition from dreaming to planning, they start to shape their trip by selecting a destination and organising the finer details. In this crucial stage, your role as a tour operator is to blend inspiration with practical guidance, showcasing both the captivating experiences awaiting them and the seamless journey you can provide.

Highlighting the expertise of your team, from knowledgeable tour guides to enthusiastic locals, builds confidence and trust in your brand as the premier choice for their travel experiences. Your objective is to not only capture their interest but to become a vital resource that guides them smoothly towards booking with you.

For multi-day tours, leveraging an automated email series, engaging videos, and targeted ads can be highly effective. Use these tools to spotlight your team, guides, and the local communities that travellers will encounter. Personalising this content is key, as your team will be spending several days or even weeks with your customers. Showcasing their friendliness, approachability, and expertise helps to create a connection, increasing the likelihood of an initial booking, repeat bookings and advocacy for your business.

Emphasising flexible cancellation policies and guarantees is also crucial. For example, allowing customers to secure their booking with a small deposit and offering the flexibility to alter their plans up to 30-60 days before the tour date can greatly influence their decision-making process. Such flexibility can significantly enhance their confidence in booking with you.

For day tours, the decision-making process is often rapid, as customers typically book in-destination. To address this, focus on showcasing your tour guides through engaging videos and highlighting positive reviews. Ensure that your landing pages cater to both dreaming and planning phases, facilitating swift decisions from travellers who may be considering their options on the spot.

Flexible cancellation policies remain important even for day tours. Make these terms clear from the beginning, particularly since many customers book tours for the same day or the next.

Additionally, some customers may bookmark your experiences

before arriving at the destination, so ensure your content supports both pre-arrival and in-destination decision-making.

Booking

The booking stage marks a crucial turning point where your customer finalises their commitment. At this moment, a smooth and intuitive booking experience is essential. A streamlined process not only secures reservations but also builds trust and satisfaction, setting the foundation for a memorable journey.

For operators who handle enquiries, it's vital to make reaching out as effortless as possible, aligning with the preferred communication methods of your potential customers. This could include implementing an easy-to-use form on your website that captures relevant information efficiently. Offering a bookable calendar for scheduling calls at their convenience can also enhance the interaction and ensure a hassle-free experience (I highly recommend this!).

Integrating an online chat feature can be highly beneficial for addressing any remaining questions or concerns about your tours. By providing immediate assistance and clarifying any uncertainties, you help potential customers feel supported and confident as they proceed with their booking.

For those who manage online bookings, simplicity is key. Avoid overwhelming customers with excessive options or add-ons during the booking process. A complex or cluttered booking interface can deter customers, much like an overly extensive menu at a restaurant might lead to indecision or frustration.

Imagine being in a restaurant presented with an overwhelming array of choices, leaving you feeling pressured to make a quick decision. This can easily happen online as well, where too many options can lead to customers feeling overwhelmed and abandoning their booking in favour of a simpler option elsewhere.

A straightforward and user-friendly booking process is essential for boosting your conversion rates and ensuring a smooth experience for your customers.

Cancellation

While not often discussed, the cancellation stage is an inevitable part of the journey. Whether due to unforeseen circumstances or changing preferences, travellers may backtrack on their plans. Here, proactive communication and enticing offers can salvage relationships and potentially convert cancellations into future bookings.

For multi-day tours, which are typically booked well in advance, initiating an email campaign can be an effective approach. Personalised messages that acknowledge the cancellation and offer reassurance can go a long way. Additionally, offering to schedule a video call provides an opportunity to discuss any concerns and explore potential solutions together.

To incentivise rebooking, consider offering a substantial discount, such as £200 off, for those who engage in the conversation. This can make rebooking more appealing and show that you value their business. Gathering feedback from customers who cancel can also provide valuable insights into potential improvements for your offerings and customer service.

For day tours, which are usually booked in-destination, a targeted SMS strategy can be highly effective. Sending text messages with special offers or exclusive discounts can prompt customers to reconsider booking with you. It's also crucial to ensure that your cancellation policies are clear and easily accessible, offering flexibility such as full or partial refunds for cancellations made within a specific timeframe.

Since customers may bookmark your tours before arriving, timely reminders with special offers or discounts can encourage them to finalise their bookings once they are in town. Engaging with customers after cancellation by sending a thank you note and a discount code for a future tour can keep your business top-of-mind and increase the likelihood of them booking with you again.

By proactively reaching out and offering compelling incentives, you can aim to turn cancellations into opportunities for renewed engagement and increased sales.

Experiencing

As the journey unfolds, travellers immerse themselves in the experiences they've eagerly anticipated. This is where your role shifts from merely delivering a service to actively enhancing the experience. By going above and beyond, you not only meet but exceed their expectations, creating moments they'll want to share with enthusiasm.

Begin by integrating opportunities for customers to capture and share their moments directly. This could include creating dedicated photo/scenic spots that are prime for social media sharing.

Consider wearing branded T-shirts, or other memorabilia, featuring a QR code that links directly to your review platforms. This makes it easy for customers to leave feedback and share their experiences. QR codes on vehicles used during the tour or at key locations can also prompt travellers to leave reviews or book additional experiences.

Another effective tool for operators is leveraging platforms like Tip Direct, which allows customers to leave their tour guide tip and a review aided by AI, in one seamless action. This not only simplifies the process but also encourages positive feedback by making it easy for customers to show appreciation for exceptional service.

Consider offering incentives for leaving a review on the spot, such as a small discount on future bookings or a free souvenir. Make sure to ask for reviews before they leave—don't wait until they're back home.

Overall, your aim is to create memorable experiences that travellers will eagerly share. By facilitating easy sharing and review processes, and by using tools like QR codes and integrated tipping platforms, you can enhance the customer experience and boost positive reviews and referrals.

Sharing

As travellers return home, their journey doesn't end—it transitions into a new role as ambassadors for your brand. Whether through social media posts, personal anecdotes, or glowing reviews, they eagerly share their adventures, helping to amplify your reach and credibility. It's crucial to harness this enthusiasm by encouraging and facilitating their sharing, which can fuel future bookings and enhance your reputation.

To maintain and strengthen this relationship, consider sending annual reminders on the anniversary of their tour. Personalised emails featuring photos from their trip can rekindle fond memories and reinforce their positive experience with you. Alongside these nostalgic emails, include a gift card for a fixed monetary amount. This provides flexibility for future bookings and offers a convenient option for friends or family members they might want to share it with. It's a thoughtful reward that shows appreciation for their loyalty and encourages them to consider booking again or sharing the opportunity with others.

Beyond the anniversary emails, think about creating a referral programme. Offer existing customers incentives, such as discounts or special offers, for referring friends and family. You could also provide exclusive access to special events or early-bird offers for those who bring new customers to your tours. By actively promoting referrals and leveraging the enthusiasm of satisfied customers, you can turn their shared experiences into a steady stream of new bookings.

Another strategy is to integrate social sharing into your customer experience. Encourage travellers to tag your business in their social media posts and use specific hashtags. Offer to share their posts on your own channels as a way to showcase real customer experiences. You might also consider running periodic social media contests where customers can win prizes for sharing their favourite moments or stories from their trip. This not only engages your audience but also creates buzz around your brand.

Finally, don't overlook the power of follow-up surveys or feedback requests. After their initial sharing, send a follow-up message to thank them and invite them to participate in a brief survey about their experience. This can provide valuable insights for improving your services while keeping the lines of communication open for future engagement.

By nurturing ongoing relationships through personalised reminders, referral incentives, and social sharing opportunities, you'll keep your customers engaged and motivated to book again, ensuring your brand remains top of mind for their next adventure.

How to map out your own Customer Purchase Journey

Whether you're running an established business or starting a new tour company, it's essential to closely examine the customer journey and plan how you intend to engage with your customers. For those of you with an existing business, this exercise might reveal gaps in your current strategies.

If you're a new operator and don't yet have a marketing strategy, the following steps will be invaluable for laying the groundwork for your approach.

I also have a video guide available in the downloads section that you might find helpful.

Step 1: Print out each stage of the customer journey separately and pin them to your wall. Files are available in the downloads section, or use a copy of my Customer Journey Toolkit, which is available at themarketing.coach.

Step 2: Grab two different coloured Post-it Notes and a pen. Let's start with the first step in the journey: Dreaming.

Step 3: Consider your main target customer and how you currently engage with them from a marketing perspective, no matter how minor. Write each of these interactions on one colour of Post-it Notes and place them under the Dreaming section on your wall, leaving some space between each note. For now, focus solely on the types of content you provide.

Step 4: Take your second colour of Post-it Notes and write down the platforms you use to promote this content—whether it's Facebook ads, your website, an email series through MailChimp, or any other platform that you may use. Position these notes next to the content they correspond with.

Step 5: Repeat this process for the other stages of the customer journey. Document the types of content and marketing strategies you currently use, and note the platforms associated with each. Take your time to thoroughly cover each stage.

Once you've mapped out your current activities throughout the customer purchase journey, evaluate if you identify any gaps or opportunities for improvement. Ask yourself, are there any red flags or areas where you could introduce new strategies?

Final thoughts

When crafting marketing strategies, and even sales processes, it's imperative to align with the customer journey at every turn. By understanding the nuances of each stage, you can tailor your efforts to resonate with travellers at each stage. This holistic approach not only helps drive bookings, but cultivates long-term loyalty and advocacy, transforming satisfied customers into passionate advocates and ambassadors for your business.

 Download the customer journey worksheet and affix it to your wall for constant reference to each stage your customer traverses. Take a moment to identify any potential marketing gaps that may exist throughout the journey. By keeping a keen eye on these crucial touchpoints, you can ensure a seamless and engaging experience for your customers at every turn.

Alternatively, I have created a Customer Journey Toolkit, available to purchase. More details at: themarketing.coach.

Building the foundations towards a successful tour business

The truth is...
do not run a tourism business.

What I mean is that you shouldn't just run a tourism business. . . at least not in the way you think. To create a successful tours and activity business in today's marketing landscape you must become more than just a tour operator. . .

You must become a media company

By media, I mean articles, guides, videos, and anything else that adds value to people researching travel or just looking to be entertained. It's not enough to have expert product knowledge in your T&A niche if your potential customers don't know about it. Becoming a 'media company' involves putting out meaningful content about your niche to drive traffic to your website or your off-site booking channels.

Making content takes time and money, but it's the only way to make yourself visible online, and to — ultimately — make yourself more visible than your competitors. Let's look at just some of the items you should have within a marketing strategy...

- Written blogs and travel guides
- Video blogs and travel guides
- Social media management
- Facebook, Google, TikTok Ads
- Remarketing
- Email list building campaigns
- Abandonment management

As you can see, with so much of digital marketing involving the creation of content, you need to change your mindset from being just a tour provider to being a tourism media company. You have to create and put out a huge amount of content that rises above the brand clutter that is already online.

While it is great to have so many available touch points and platforms to engage with your customers, it is also easy to lose focus and for your strategy to become disjointed. Believe me, I understand how easy it can unravel. Usually this is down to two things:

- No proper marketing strategy, informed by data
- You are too quick to change your strategy.

It's extremely hard work to run your own tours and activity company, and business owners usually want to see instant results. Especially anyone who runs small, family-owned businesses.

I totally get it: cash flow is king and the money you put into marketing needs to provide clear advantages. In short, it's all about return on investment;. Because of this, sometimes perfectly worthwhile strategies are scrapped because they don't work straight away. However, where digital marketing is concerned, patience is a chief virtue.

Organic marketing takes time to build and requires a lot of patience, but it is more than worth the wait. In the meantime, however, paid ads can help you gain traction a little quicker, and this is usually one of the things my team at the Tourism Marketing Agency

(TMA) implements in the short term. Paid ads can compete for vital traffic while we work on your organic marketing. Business guru Gary Vaynerchuk swears by being more patient and, with digital marketing, he is definitely right.

To give you an example of the patience required, my own video advice series, The Digital Tourism Show, took 6-8 months and nearly 190 videos (I was doing these daily!) before it finally broke through and helped raise my own profile and generate leads. There were times where I felt like giving up, but I urged myself to keep going and I am glad I did.

Even if I haven't fully convinced you yet, I hope you'll start thinking about the admittedly strange concept of transforming your business into a media company. And, while it isn't ideal, I hope I've convinced you that patience is an incredibly important part of the process.

Will you make mistakes along the way? Of course you will. With this book, however, my hope is you will make less mistakes and create a media company you're proud of — one that just so happens to sell and promote exceptional tourism experiences.

What is a brand?

When I ask someone "what is a brand?" the typical responses are:

1. My logo
2. My company image
3. My products

Branding is about creating your identity, your ethos; it's about defining how you perceive your company and, more importantly, how you want your customers to perceive you.

In the process of defining your brand, you'll make many of the most important decisions you'll ever make for your company – and it can make you stand out from the competition! However, ultimately, it's not as simple as deciding how you'd like to be perceived; the consumer market, your customers, will also determine who you are as a brand, and the truth of that branding will determine your perceived value. A brand is not your logo, a product or service. . .

You do not create or own your brand

Let me repeat: you do not own your brand. In fact, some readers with their own company might not even have a brand yet. People, your consumers, create and own your brand. You become a brand once you have become a trusted company.

Once you have customers that follow your every move and sing your praises from the rooftops. This trust comes from meeting (and beating) expectations. Then and only then do you have a good brand.

You see, all you can do is try to persuade people to believe in your brand, but with a little thought and planning, ANY company can achieve this. . . even yours.

Ask yourself this...

- Where is your brand in relation to your competition?
- Are you offering different or better products or services?
- Can you target a different audience with similar products?
- Can you fill a current niche market or create a new one?

Is there a group or are there groups of people out there whose needs are not being met?

Clever marketing makes consumers try a product for a variety of reasons. Many of us will try a different product because of a special offer – but think about it: how often have you been disappointed by a product that was significantly cheaper than its competition? As my mother always says, "Buy cheap, buy twice".

In the long-term, it's better to have a brand people trust as, when people learn their lessons about buying cheaper and inferior products, they will always gravitate back to better quality brands.

Once people have decided they like a product, and it does exactly what is says it does, and is priced fairly – then you usually have a customer for life!

Remember that your brand positioning is usually determined by consumers comparing it to your competitors' brands. Always keep an eye on what your competitors are doing, and strive to do it better.

No matter how good or established your products or services are, the way the world is viewing and buying experiences is changing constantly and it is opening new markets for those in a position to take advantage of them. To make your brand stand out your business must master the four disciplines of branding. . .

- Your brand path
- Your brand voice
- Your brand personality
- Your brand identity

Mastering these four disciplines will make the process of building your business far easier.

Finding your path

When you go on an adventure walking tour, you take time to plan your journey. What equipment you need, provisions, where you will camp, or glamp, along the predefined route you selected. This is no different from running your business.

If you wish your business to grow and succeed you first have to know which path you need to take before setting out on your journey.

With a little research, you can define your core values, mission, and goals. Determine your audience(s) and analyse the competition. Establish your USP (Unique Selling Point) and what makes your company stand out from the rest. Why you? Why would someone want to buy from you versus someone else who sells the same product or experience?

I bet some of you will already want to put down "we are the cheapest". Don't. This is not really a USP as anyone can say this. If you compete on price you will always lose. Someone will always do it cheaper, driving your business, sector and cashflow down. If you compete on experience, exceptional quality and service, you can charge whatever you want.

In order to get to where you want to go, you need to make sure you're heading in the right direction. Don't just think of the here and now. Where do you want your brand to be in five years from now? What about in 10 years?

They say it takes five years to establish a strong business. If this is true, why do so many business owners only think about the short term? For example, many tour and activity businesses concentrate on putting something out in the public domain as soon as possible without thinking how this may affect their long-term business.

If you do not plan your brand path properly, you will end up with a poorly conceived, inconsistent, ineffective brand with no direction. And guess what? All this does is give the impression of an unattractive, poorly run business. And the only path that will be left open to you is the one towards insolvency.

Okay, that might seem extreme, but from my experience, it can definitely go like this if a company isn't careful.

Now... take a deep breath and relax. Think about where you wish to be in five years time.

1. You may wish to become a franchise.
2. You may wish to build a business that you can sell on.
3. You may wish to build a business that simply provides you with a certin lifestyle
4. You may want to become the number one brand in your niche.

Whatever it is, take the time to plan it right and you will take your first steps along the right path.

With this in mind, and without further ado, please may I introduce you to Carol and Atef of Sina Tours...

Meet Carol & Atef of Sina Tours

Carol and Atef are the heart and soul of Sina Tours.

Atef started working in the tourism sector when he was 22, and, eventually, in 1988, he borrowed some money to start his own tour company. From the beginning, he was highly successful, and the knowledge, expertise, and contacts he built up helped him survive through the many challenges faced by tourism in Egypt. Then in 2014, an enormous stroke of good fortune happened... he met Carol.

Although born and brought up in Scotland (many of the best people come from here!), Carol has had a lifelong passion for Egypt, fuelled by some watercolour paintings brought back by her great-great-aunt who went there in 1910-ish. That said, she didn't expect that at the age of 49 she would end up married to an Egyptian and living in Cairo... but that's exactly what happened.

Her first few years in Egypt were spent in the education sector, but when the company she worked for shut down in 2020, it seemed the perfect opportunity to fulfil a lifelong tourism dream by joining Atef in the tourism business.

Also, as a side hustle, Carol setup Literary Tours in Egypt, a company that specialised in tours in Egypt that focused on the works of great novelists from around the world, including Agatha Christie and Rosie Thomas.

Meeting Atef has turned out to be a match made in heaven. Atef has an extraordinary ability to source anything; this is due to his knowledge, experience, and contacts. Meanwhile, Carol's leadership, organisational and technical skills enables them to take advantage of the many new opportunities that technology has brought the tourism sector; it also helps them cater to the many bespoke needs of their customers.

So, this is Carol and Atef, but what about Sina Tours? What do they stand for? What are their values?

Let's find out by conducting a brand workshop...

Who are Sina Tours... really?

Who Sina Tours actually are, where they currently sit in their market, and how they see themselves are all such important questions to answer. Without the answers to these questions of identity, the brand would be directionless and without the backbone required for all marketing and communications going forward.

For those of you who read my previous book, you will remember that I had a whole brand workshop section you can conduct to help answer these and many more questions. I took Carol and Atef through this process, individually, so that I could get a sense of what each of them thought about their business. Doing this in isolation was important as it meant they weren't overly influenced by each other's answers.

When you conduct your own brand workshop (you can download the worksheets from the link at the start of this book), please make sure you and your team do this in their own time and by themselves. Once you all answer the questions, come together to collate everyone's opinions about the business. I wouldn't be surprised if most people in your business have different views and ideas about where and what your brand is.

Next, I will highlight the answers from Carol and Atef. Then I will assess what I think about their brand.

Q1. What is your USP?

With this question, I wanted to ascertain what they feel their unique selling point (USP) is.

From the answers above, this tells me that they offer unique experiences that no one else can deliver and that they have a huge amount of experience. I also got the sense that Carol is more focused on the consumer's wants and dreams while Atef is a little more focused on how his experience and contacts can deliver to enhance that experience. Both compliment each other very well and will have huge benefits on the success of the business.

Q2. What are the features and benefits of your service/product offering?

Expanding on the USPs, what makes you different from every other business?

Carol

- Over 30 years of experience creating tours in Egypt
- Unparalleled knowledge of what to see and do in Egypt
- Extensive understanding of what Western European and North American tourists are looking for
- Highest levels of service to ensure the comfort and safety of all our customers

Atef

- Over 33 years experience in the industry
- Contacts across Egypt relating to everything in the whole tourism industry, including government departments. My hand is everywhere. Hotels, transport, all sights, guides
- Can get access to things other agencies can't (legally!)
- Arrange short tours right up to several weeks long including everything or just the bits the customers want

It is clear that both Carol and Atef have a huge amount of experience between them and would be able to help deliver experiences that really no one else can.

Carol has a strong skill set in talking with Western European and the North American markets. Safety is also an important aspect for Carol and something she feels needs to come across in some of the communications.

Atef, on the other hand, due to his experience and contacts, can provide access to many parts of Egypt that no other operator can provide. This helps create truly unique experiences for the consumer. Atef is a man who gets things done.

Overall, it's all about bending over backwards for their customers and over delivering.

Q3. What are the value/benefits you bring to customers' lives?

How do you enrich your customers' lives? You must deliver an experience they will not forget. If you feel you don't, then you are maybe in the wrong line of business.

Carol

- See Egypt exactly how you want to
- Access to places other operators can't access
- Focus on safety and security
- Fully qualified and licensed Egyptologist guides, trained by a foreigner (me)
- Ability to procure practically anything

Atef

- Over 33 years experience in the industry
- Contacts across Egypt relating to everything in the whole tourism industry, including government departments. My hand is everywhere. Hotels, transport, all sights, guides
- Can get access to things other agencies can't (legally!)
- Arrange short tours right up to several weeks long including everything or just the bits the customers want

Safety and flexibility are what these answers suggest to me. Being able to be super flexible, catering to the consumers' needs — this is a strong USP.

Both Carol and Atef are available if that consumer runs into any issues during their trip so this ties in with the safety aspect that is important to Carol and highlights to the consumer that they are available 24/7 to personally solve any concerns that may arise. Another USP!

Carol also made the point that she is fully qualified and 'licensed'. The latter is a huge aspect as in Egypt there are many un-licensed operators that can't provide the same security and insurances that Sina Tours can.

Q4. What does your business/product do?

If you had just 60 seconds to explain your product to a customer, what would you highlight?

Carol
We work with our customers to understand their interests and create unique tours designed especially for them. Egypt has a rich and vibrant history going back thousands of years, and it can be difficult to decide what to see and do in the time you have available. We combine our unmatched knowledge of Egypt with an understanding of what customers expect from their holiday to create something special that nobody else will have experienced.

We apply the highest standards to all our tours, whether a half day tour of the Pyramids or a month-long grand tour of Egypt.

Atef

I have a great job. I get to arrange holidays for people and to see people happy because they've seen things they have dreamt about their whole lives. To be successful at doing this is the biggest thing that motivates people.

Q5. What problem do you solve, or what 'need' do you meet?

What is the purpose of your existence (other than to make money)? If a business is not solving a problem or fulfilling a need for customers, then it will fail.

Carol

We want as many people as possible in the world to be able to experience the wonders of Egypt, in the best way that suits their circumstances.

Atef

I make people's dreams come true in a way that gives them memories for a lifetime.

Basically these two questions confirm what we saw earlier. It is all about the consumer and how they can make their time in Egypt as unique and as special as possible.

Carol and Atef are the 'Mr & Mrs' of Egypt! For me, these guys are the brand and should be the face of Sina Tours.

Q6. List up to ten of your main competitors

What do you like and dislike about them? It pays to know who you're competing against and what the industry norms are. Know them, learn from them, but don't copy them. Do your own thing! Pay attention to each competitor's website, product/service, marketing, and brand image likes and dislikes.

Quick note: *For the sake of the other companies, and to help protect Sina Tours, I will not show who they feel are competitors to their brand. With this, I asked what their likes and dislikes are for each brand they selected.*

What was clear from this part of the workshop, is that the quality of the other brands was fairly poor. From how their brands look, the content, the website etc, it was all a bit old-fashioned and did not scream quality, nor did it instil trust.

Atef's commented on one competitor as follows:

Atef

The website is really fake because they are not a travel company but a collection of individual tour guides who

What this says to me is that Sina Tours are 'legit', have full insurance and that consumers need to do their due diligence when selecting a company in Egypt. This must be a page on the site to convey the trust element of the brand while showing that they care deeply for their customers' well-being.

Q7. Why should your potential customers buy from you instead of from your competitors?

Consumers today are spoilt for choice. Expand on your unique selling point (USP) and highlight any other aspect that makes you unique.

Carol
- Book and pay online using secure methods
- Can contact a member of the team any time before and after booking and during the holiday
- We understand what foreign tourists want and need
- We understand and address conc erns around health and security

Atef

Ability to be flexible and my huge knowledge of Egypt, and being able to arrange anything at any time because of my contacts and relationships.

Being able to offer a complete and very high level of service and being available to the customer during their whole holiday. It's my number one priority to make sure they have a great time and their dreams come true. If anything goes wrong, I'll be there to sort it out. I can and will do anything to help make sure they feel safe and they are safe.

This screams value, expertise, flexibility, and trustworthiness. They understand their customers and want to make sure they have an amazing, safe experience.

Throughout the questions so far, you can probably see Carol is very much about taking care of the customer while Atef, who also cares about his customers, is about delivering the experience in the best way possible.

Q8. Describe your ideal customer?

Who do you feel is your target demographic(s)? This is important as this will shape all marketing decisions going forward.

Carol
How old are they, where do they live, and what is their profession?

- They live in Western Europe, the Americas, Australia
- Early 20s to old

What is their budget?

Enough to have a really good holiday

What personality do they have?

Interested in history, enquiring mind, open to learning new things, quite adventurous.

If you could pick one famous person to be a brand ambassador to promote your brand... who would it be?

- Kara Cooney
- Alice Roberts
- Brian Cox

Atef

How old are they, where do they live, and what is their profession?

- 40-60 - Latin America, America, any job

What is their budget?

I prefer not too rich but enough money to have a good holiday. Very rich are unfriendly and hard to satisfy.

What personality do they have?

Talkative, friendly, joking, love Egypt, interested & knowledgeable about the history.

This was super interesting. Carol felt the target audience was early 20s and above while Atef felt it was more 40 to 60 year olds. This disconnect in how you understand how the wrong demographic can creep into how you market a business, which will confuse anyone you are trying to target.

Atef's reasoning was that he felt this age group are more interested in history and culture, have more disposable income (normally), and are more mature and 'less demanding'.

Carol's reasoning was that she felt Egypt does attract people of all ages, but on reflection she agreed with Atef (which does not happen often… her words!) that the slightly older demographic is more ideal.

People who travel to Egypt tend to have a little more disposable income and are interested in the culture and history of the country.

The last question was a bit of fun. If money was not an issue, which actor would be the face of your brand. Mel Gibson I felt was an odd choice but apparently he is huge in Egypt because of the film Braveheart… Apparently Egyptians love Scotland!

Q9. Share five adjectives or words that you feel best describe your company

The words you choose should convey a lot of meaning regarding how you see yourself, or how you want to see yourself.

Carol
- Flexible
- Expert
- Trustworthy
- Friendly
- Professional

Atef
- Punctual
- Integrity
- Caring
- Friendly
- Straightforward

This was interesting as only friendly was said by both Carol and Atef, but what again is clear is that they are both focused on making it a fantastic experience at each interaction with their customers.

Workshop conclusions

To determine the best brand for Sina Tours, we spent a long time during the workshop discussing the findings of each question and the list of adjectives both Carol and Ataf associate with Sina Tours. How did Carol and Atef want to be perceived? What were their overall goals?

After a short discussion, Carol and Atef decided on the following five adjectives:

1. Friendly
2. Professional
3. Transparent
4. Personable
5. Trustworthy
6. Adaptable

Ok that's six, but we feel the extra one was required to encompass everything Sina Tours is and should be about. These adjectives will form the spine of Sina Tours, how all communications should be going forward, and how staff are to treat consumers.

We also generated a strong idea about the target demographics; this gives us a head start on how we can start thinking about the strategies we will create for Sina Tours.

Whether you are a start-up or an existing business, it is so important to go through this full brand workshop. For new businesses, it can help you walk along the right path to achieve your goals. For established businesses, it can help guide you back on the right path if you feel you have perhaps strayed too far off what you originally envisioned.

Now that we know how and what we want Sina Tours to stand for, we will take a look at how they should brand themselves. Is Sina Tours the right name? Does that convey what Carol and Atef are all about?

Let's find out.

Now it is your turn...
Download the worksheets and have everyone in your business fill out the questions. Find out where your business currently sits and what your team actually thinks. Make it anonymous so that they can speak their minds.

Whether you're on your own or doing this as a team, I bet you will find out a few surprises. I suspect some of you will struggle to answer some of the questions, and that is not a bad thing. It is always hard to talk about yourself. However, talking about yourself makes you sit back and really take stock of what you think of your business... or at least what you thought your business stood for.

Birth of a new brand

After the brand workshop, it became clear to all that the name 'Sina Tours' did not reflect the personality of what the brand should be. Although Sina means 'treasure', the brand was too 'cold' and came across as a typical travel agent rather than a personalised, consumer-focused experience. The website was also very dated.

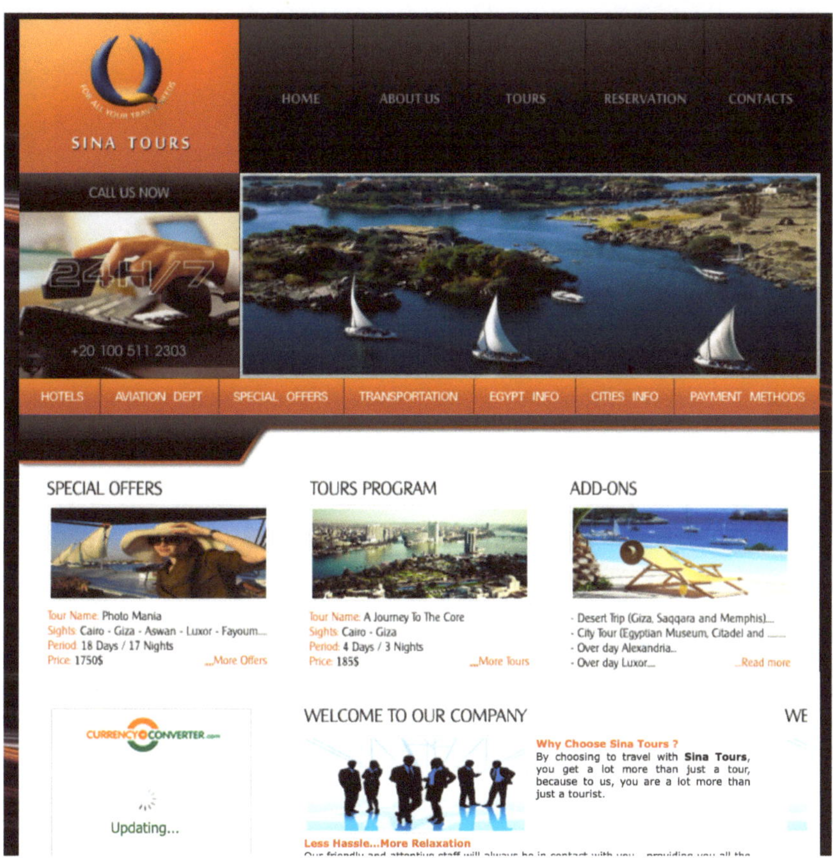

When thinking about a new brand look and feel, it should be focused around Carol and Atef as they are the team that have the expertise and deliver the experiences. They are Mr & Mrs Egypt!

When considering a new brand, you have to take a few things into consideration:

1. Is it absolutely necessary?
2. If rebranding, how will this affect other aspects?
   - Rebranding vehicles
   - Website
   - Clothing
   - Shop front/signage
   - Everything!
3. What benefits will it bring?
4. What negative connotations may it bring?
5. How will it affect SEO rankings?
6. Are domain names available!

I could go on. You must weigh up the pros and cons of a complete rebrand before undertaking such a task. There is a lot more to it than just updating a logo.

Using the colour wheel method

We are now going to see if the Sina Tours brand can stand out from the crowd. I've invented a simple way of illustrating how you sit alongside your competitors' logos by using a colour wheel.

Take screenshots from around 8-10 competitors, and your own logo, print out each of these and cut them out into individual logos. if you would rather not print them, you can use software like photoshop to do this instead.

Now, place the logos around the colour-wheel to the colours that match the predominant colour used in their logos. Do you see any pattern to how your competitors are using colour? Let's look at Sina Tours...

Nearly every one of them, along with Sina Tours, had poor branding and did nothing to 'excite' the consumer — a typical trait, it seems, for Egyptian travel companies.

Travco's brand logo, for example, looks like they are an airline rather than an experience provider. Blue Sky Travel's brand logo looks like a Japanese travel company, with the icon looking like a paper lantern you would see outside a traditional Ryokan (Japanese Inn). It is meant to represent the Nile using the B, S and T of the brand name, but it simply does not work. Memphis Tours' brand logo, while the best of the bunch, still misses the mark. They are a tour company, so why have a plane in the logo?

This is just a small selection but most we found were along similar lines.

You will see, there are a lot of terrible brand logos out there that don't shout 'Egypt Experiences'. This is not a bad thing as it gives Sina Tours a lot of scope to come up with something that truly stands out.

Developing a logo

When it comes to creating a logo, you must adhere to some basics to make sure you create something that will work on many formats and at different sizes. Far too often, I've seen logos with intricate designs that simply don't print well at small sizes. Also, think of your logo as a badge. It should be a self-contained element that doesn't take up too much real estate. Let's look at elements you must follow.

Avoid following trends

When Apple designed the iOS system, every designer wanted to design a logo with gradients and drop shadows. Fast forward to 2019 and that look is dated. This is because design trends last only for a short time. You must create a logo that is contemporary and that will stand the test of time.

Look at Nike's swoosh. It's simple and it can work on any medium, against any colour.

Create your logo in black and white FIRST

When designing a logo it should look as equally good in black and white as it does in colour. You may also need to print your logo in a monochrome format when publishing in newspapers or when your logo is white on a solid colour.

Designing in black and white first helps you see how a logo looks more clearly as you do not get distracted by pretty colours. This also helps highlight any design issues.

It must scale – and don't use Photoshop!!!

Your logo should look crisp and sharp whether it's the size of a postage stamp or draped over the side of a building. Logos with small design elements will only get lost at smaller sizes. Remember, your logo could also be printed on pens or stitched on your company polo shirt, as well as on stationery and brochures. It should also be legible from various distances.

Never, ever use Photoshop. Logos should be designed in vector format as this format can scale to any size. Scaling logos that have been designed in Photoshop can make them look pixelated at large sizes. Vector logos are also easier to change if used on different colour combinations.

Adobe Illustrator is the industry standard for vector logos so make sure whoever is designing your logo uses this format.

Use the vision test with your logo designs

Another method I created was the vision test. Print your logo in the middle of an A4 sheet of paper. Pin it to your wall. Stand at the furthest away point at the other side of your room.

Can you still make out your logo? Still readable? If so, good job. Your logo should be readable from a distance as it could be used on vehicles, billboards, clothing and other materials that customers may see on the move. If it is not readable, scrap it and start again.

Be minimalistic

Remove all the excessive elements from a logo. Keep only those elements that are just enough to convey a message. If your logo is messy, you will just be seen as a chaotic company.

Also avoid small details in your logo. If your logo is intricate then at small sizes these details will be lost or disappear entirely.

Although a logo icon can and does work well, there is also no need to design an icon to go with your logo. A good typeface can be more than enough. A simple but strong logo will better catch the eye of your customers than something they need to spend five minutes studying to find out what it is.

Also, choose no more than two typefaces and two colours within your logo. This helps give the impression as being more professional and helps with printing further down the line. Keep it simple.

Create brand guidelines

Armed with all the information from finding your path, voice and personality, take all of this, with your logo, and create a brand guideline book that will help you and your team stay consistent. It is also handy when others use your logo as you can set some rules that they must abide by.

Your brand guidelines should include the design and layout of key materials, like your stationery, email signatures, typefaces and image use — to name just a few.

I have included a few example brand guidelines documents in the resources section to give you an idea how this should look. Your designer should be able to create this for you.

To summarise, your logo...

1. needs to work in a singular colour
2. needs to be scalable, therefore simple
3. needs to be unique and different from competitors
4. should be used in all different compositions and applications
5. needs to tell the brand's message
6. should be easy to remember

The Sina Tours brand logo

While developing brand logos, the first iterations were along the lines of what I was trying to achieve. Make them clean, easy to understand, and make them stand out at various sizes. Here are the first couple of designs I created:

While I liked these, they still seemed a little 'typical' to me, but I love the colour scheme of gold and dark grey/black. Both company names also seemed a little too generic for my liking. It was important to highlight that they are a 30+ year company so I added 'EST 1988' to the logo. Things like this give consumers confidence.

The logos here are also in keeping with the minimalistic style I mentioned. Strong in how they look, but they would also work across various mediums at any size.

I wanted something a little more personal to Carol and Atef. Something that drew on their experience, their love of Egypt while staying true to the brand voice we wanted to develop.

With all this in mind, I took what I liked from the first iterations and created what I felt Carol and Atef needed.

Please may I introduce you to Mr & Mrs Egypt:

I kept the colour scheme, the established date and added a tagline 'Fully Custom Egyptian Experiences'. The use of Egyptian cats was something I felt was unique and have not seen used within the travel space as it tends to be elements like pyramids and the Sphinx. The two cats also tie in nicely with representing Carol and Atef and the fact they also love cats, whom have made frequent appearances in video calls...

Everything about the final logo just 'screamed' Carol, Atef, and the focus of the brand voice. They are people who get things done in Egypt and make dreams come true. They are Mr & Mrs Egypt!

Let's now look at the new logo beside the others:

It is never a good idea to have one of your customers cry in a call, but that is what Carol did (in a good way) and that reaction told me that we had hit the nail on the head and that we were seeing the rebirth of their business. For a brand development expert like me, it was an exciting prospect.

Brand logo conclusions

Creating a logo is such an important aspect that many get wrong. Many small businesses end up asking a friend who 'knows Photoshop' to create them a quick logo because of budget restraints. I get it. However, more often than not it hinders your business in many ways you don't realise.

When you design your logo, it must come with purpose, with a good story, and with solid reasoning behind it. Remember, the logo represents your company to potential customers. It must stand out and fit the ethos of your business. If your brand logo comes across as 'lost', how will the rest of your business be seen?

Mr & Mrs Egypt now have the foundation of a good brand logo as well as a voice and purpose. We now must take these elements into all aspects of their future marketing.

Auditing Sina Tours content footprint

Conducting a comprehensive content audit is crucial for understanding the current state of your website and identifying areas for improvement. For Sina Tours, this process has highlighted several key issues that need to be addressed to enhance both user experience and search engine optimisation (SEO).

A content audit is essentially a thorough examination of all the content on your website. This process involves evaluating how well your content is performing, identifying gaps, and ensuring that it aligns with your business goals. For Sina Tours, this audit focused on three main areas:

Content optimisation for search

This involves ensuring that your website is speaking the language of search engines like Google. Elements such as meta titles, meta descriptions, headers (H1, H2, H3), and internal linking all play critical roles in how Google reads and ranks your site.

User experience (UX) and user journey

UX focuses on how easily visitors can navigate your website and find the information they need. A well-structured site with clear pathways is more likely to keep users engaged and encourage them to take action, such as booking a tour.

Content marketing

This includes the creation and distribution of valuable, relevant content to attract and retain your target audience. Regular updates, blogs, and guides not only engage your audience but also improve your site's ranking on search engines.

The content audit for Sina Tours revealed several areas that require significant improvement:

Outdated website design

The current website was old-fashioned, which could deter potential customers. A modern, visually appealing site is essential to compete with other Egypt tour operators.

Lack of optimisation for search engines

Meta titles and descriptions on the current site were not optimised for search, which impacts the site's visibility on search engine results pages (SERPs). For example, meta titles should follow a standard format that includes keyword-rich phrases and the brand name (e.g., "Luxury Tours of Egypt | Sina Tours").

Missing headers (H1, H2, H3)

The absence of headers like H1, H2, and H3 across the site is a major issue. These headers are essential for SEO as they help Google understand the structure and content of your pages. Every page should have a clear H1 tag, with additional H2s and H3s to break down the content further.

Sparse content

The body content on the website is minimal, giving both users and Google very little information to work with. More detailed content is necessary to convey the value of the tours and services and to improve SEO performance.

Lack of internal links

There are almost no internal links on the current site. Internal linking is crucial as it helps guide users through your website and signals to Google which pages are important.

Weak UX and user journey

The user journey on the site is not clearly defined. For instance, the menu options are confusing, and the secondary menu bar offers too many choices, which can overwhelm users. The site needs to be restructured to create a more intuitive and user-friendly experience.

Content marketing deficiencies

There is no evidence of content marketing efforts, such as blogs or travel guides, on the current site. Regularly updated content is important not only for engaging their audience but also for improving your SEO rankings. Starting a blog and producing travel guides should be a priority once the new website is built.

By addressing the issues identified, we can significantly enhance their online presence, making it easier for potential customers to find and book their experiences. A well-optimised site with strong content and a seamless user journey will not only improve your search engine rankings but also increase customer engagement and conversions.

Conducting your own content audit

To carry out a content audit like the one performed for Sina Tours, follow these steps:

1. Inventory your content

Start by creating a list of all the content on your website. This includes every page, blog post, landing page, and downloadable resource. Tools like Screaming Frog or Sitemap Generator can help automate this process by crawling your site and generating a comprehensive inventory of your content.

2. Assess content performance

Use tools like Google Analytic to evaluate how each piece of content is performing. Look at metrics such as page views, bounce rates, and time on page to understand user engagement. Additionally, Hotjar or Crazy Egg can provide heatmaps and session recordings to see how visitors interact with your content, offering deeper insights into user behaviour.

3. Evaluate SEO elements

Review the SEO components of each page, including meta titles, descriptions, headers, and internal links. Ensure that each page is optimised with relevant keywords. SEMrush and Ahrefs are powerful tools that can help you analyse and optimise these elements by providing keyword data, tracking your rankings, and offering suggestions for improvement.

4. Review user experience

Navigate your website as if you were a potential customer. Is it easy to find information? Are the pathways clear? Identify any barriers that might prevent users from converting. Tools like GT Metrix can also help you assess page load times and overall site performance.

5. Identify content gaps

Look for areas where your site lacks content. Are there topics your target audience is searching for that you haven't covered? Are your key selling points clearly communicated? BuzzSumo can be a valuable tool for content gap analysis, helping you identify popular topics within your niche that you may not have covered. SEMrush's Content Gap tool can also show you keywords your competitors rank for that you don't.

6. Make a plan for improvement

Based on your findings, create a plan to update and optimise your content. This might include rewriting pages, adding new blog posts, or restructuring your site for better UX.

Using these tools in your content audit process will not only streamline the task but also provide you with actionable insights to improve your content and website's performance.

Keyword research for Sina Tours

Keyword research is a fundamental aspect of any marketing strategy, and for Sina Tours, it's crucial to ensure that your website, ads and brand voice is optimised to attract the right audience.

Keywords are the specific terms and phrases that potential customers use when searching for travel experiences online. By identifying and strategically incorporating these keywords into your content, you can significantly enhance your website's visibility on search engines, driving more relevant traffic to your site.

Conducting keyword research involves several steps, each designed to refine your understanding of what potential customers are searching for and how you can align your content with their queries.

1. Start with broad topics

Begin by brainstorming broad topics related to your business. For Sina Tours, these could include "luxury tours in Egypt," "cultural experiences in Egypt," or "Nile River cruises." These broad topics serve as a foundation for identifying more specific keywords.

2. Generate keyword ideas

Use tools like SEMrush, Ahrefs, or Google Keyword Planner to generate a list of potential keywords related to your broad topics. These tools provide data on search volume (how often a keyword is searched) and keyword difficulty (how hard it is to rank for a keyword). Focus on keywords that have a high search volume but are not too competitive.

3. Analyse competitor keywords

Look at what keywords your competitors are targeting. Tools like SEMrush, Ahrefs and SpyFu can help you analyse competitor websites to identify the keywords they are ranking for. This can give you insight into potential keywords you might have overlooked and help you stay competitive.

4. Refine your keyword list

Narrow down your list by focusing on keywords that are highly relevant to your business and have a good balance of search volume and competition. Prioritise long-tail keywords—these are longer, more specific phrases (e.g., "best luxury Nile River cruise for couples") that typically have lower competition and higher conversion rates.

5. Assign keywords to content

Once you have a refined list of keywords, assign them to specific pages on your website. Each page should be optimised for one primary keyword and several secondary keywords. This helps Google understand the relevance of your content and rank your pages accordingly.

6. Track and adjust

After implementing your keyword strategy, use tools like Google Search Console and SEMrush to track your rankings and traffic for each keyword. Regularly review this data to adjust your strategy as needed, ensuring that you continue to target the most effective keywords.

When my team undertakes keyword research at my agency, we go far beyond just the top 25 keywords (unlike most agencies). We dive deep into the data, meticulously analysing a wide range of keywords and compiling our findings into a comprehensive Google Sheet for our clients. These keywords are not only crucial for SEO and content strategy but also serve as a foundation for Google search campaigns. Essentially, they form the backbone of all future marketing efforts.

 You can find an example of our detailed keyword research document for Sina Tours in the downloads section.

Building the Mr & Mrs Egypt website

The next step in laying the foundations was the website. It's crucial that the website not only aligns with the brand voice and the look and feel of the brand logo, but also ensures a seamless purchase journey for the customer.

While I won't delve into website development in this section (which I extensively cover in my first book), I will discuss some of the choices we made for the Mr & Mrs Egypt website and the rationale behind them. But first, let's address a couple of frequently asked questions...

Should you build a bespoke site or use an off the shelf solution?

I'll be straightforward here... In my opinion, most of you reading this book should never consider paying for a bespoke website. It's an expense you can do without. Whether you're a sole proprietor or managing a team across various locations, there are excellent WordPress templates available for less than $70 that can deliver a superb website.

I'm not exaggerating when I say that I regularly hear from tour operators and business owners who regret spending thousands on a site not fit for purpose. They struggle with updates or face exorbitant charges from developers/agencies for even minor changes.

I can confidently assert this as someone who currently runs a marketing agency where we built bespoke websites for companies like Gray Line. However, I sold that aspect of the business because I foresaw the trajectory of the web development landscape. It was increasingly difficult to justify high costs for websites when affordable solutions were available.

The rise of cost-effective WordPress themes, as well as booking platforms offering free websites, signalled the inevitable. Profiting from web development was becoming increasingly challenging.

Now, my agency includes a website for free with our marketing packages. This ensures that the businesses we assist can hit the ground running with a high-performing website that can be deployed rapidly.

For those familiar with my work, it's no secret that I endorse the Travel Tour WordPress theme available on ThemeForest (https://bit.ly/4cZBN6I). It's user-friendly, easy to update, and priced at only £69 at the time of writing. It's compatible with various booking platforms and even includes its own basic booking platform if preferred. If they provided an affiliate scheme I would be a rich man now.

AI will revolutionise web development once more. By providing criteria to platforms like ChatGPT, a site can be coded in seconds. While basic, it's a glimpse into the future of web development. Soon, you'll install WordPress, input information, and have a site generated without relying on templates. This is coming.

Should you own your website?

Again, in my opinion... yes!

I simply prefer having control over my 'shop window'. Your website serves as the foundation for all your online activities, be it marketing or sales, so relinquishing control of it doesn't sit well with me.

While services like Wix, Squarespace, and even Fareharbor offer an easy route to getting online, my experience suggests they're not ideal for SEO, content updates can be cumbersome, and incorporating tracking plugins can be challenging or impossible. Additionally, if you decide to switch services, you'd need to rebuild the entire site rather than simply changing hosting providers. There are too many restrictions for my taste.

So, if you ask me, I'd always advocate for owning your own site as it offers flexibility and greater control.

Key decisions for the Mr & Mrs Egypt website

As Sina Tours was rebranding to Mr & Mrs Egypt and the brand voice completely changed, the business was in essence starting from scratch again. There were no online reviews and the information on the current website was not fit for purpose. Because of this, we were limited in what we could repurpose so everything was created from the ground up, content included.

One thing we did not need to worry about was a booking platform as everything was enquiry based. This is normal for multi-day experiences as customers tend to want to speak to someone before parting with large sums of cash. They need to feel reassured and can trust the company to deliver excellence. Online booking in this space is growing, but enquires is still the main sales channel.

With the website, the priority was to highlight the extensive experience Carol and Atef bring to the table (over 30 years). Their knowledge, experience, and personalities needed to shine through to build trust with their target audience, convincing them that this was the brand to deliver the experiences they craved. Video is one of the best mediums for this, but it wasn't easy. Carol and Atef were initially uncomfortable in front of the camera, a common issue among tour operators that I find perplexing. Tour guides present to customers daily, so why is a camera intimidating? A camera never judges.

Eventually, I persuaded them, and we now have a wealth of video footage to use across various platforms. More on that later.

Imagery was also crucial. We relied heavily on photos of landmarks and scenes around Egypt, as there weren't many with customers at this early stage. However, we found enough to create an appealing website that resonated with their audience.

Content was going to be a main driver organically, so a dedicated travel guide area (blog) was essential for any travel site.

The tour page is arguably the most critical page on the site. It's the make-or-break page for bookings or enquiries. Designing the perfect tour page is vital for tour operators. Drawing from extensive experience and research, I've identified the key elements that make a tour page effective.

Let's dive into what the tour page should contain:

1. Clear navigation

Top Navigation: Ensure your navigation is intuitive. This helps visitors quickly find what they're looking for and enhances user experience.

2. Descriptive title

Tour Name: Highlight the main attraction, whether it's the Eiffel Tower or Notre Dame. Incorporate relevant keywords to boost SEO. As an example, for Mr & Mrs Egypt, one tour is called 'Red Sea & Ancient Egypt Historical Tour'

3. Tour highlights

Duration & Quick Details: Display essential information like the tour's length, maximum guests, and availability. This gives a snapshot of the tour's specifics.

Visual Gallery: Showcase a gallery of high-quality images, offering a visual taste of the experience.

4. Booking panel

Sticky Side Panel: As visitors scroll, the booking panel should remain visible on the side. This ensures the 'Book Now' or enquiry form option is always within reach, enhancing the chances of conversion.

5. Detailed itinerary

Brief Overview: Start with a concise introduction, highlighting the tour's main attractions.

Comprehensive Breakdown: Especially for multi-day tours, provide a day-by-day breakdown. Even for day tours, outline the main stops or attractions.

6. Interactive map

Route or Pickup Point: Embed a map, from Google, to show the tour route or the pickup point. This offers clarity and aids in planning.

7. Reviews and trust signal

Customer Reviews: Showcase genuine customer feedback. This builds trust and offers social proof.

Tour Specific FAQs: Address common queries. Limit this to the most relevant questions to avoid overwhelming the visitor.

8. Related tours

Tag-based Suggestions: Display tours related to the one the visitor is viewing. If they're looking at a 'food tour', suggest other food-related tours. This encourages further exploration.

9. Clean design

Contrasting Text: Opt for easily readable text, like black on a white background. Avoid over-complicating with too many colours.

Mobile Optimization: Ensure the layout is mobile-friendly. Consider placing the booking panel at the top for mobile users for easy access, or have a floating button at the bottom of the page so when clicked, it takes the user to the booking widget.

10. Sub-menu for easy navigation

Jump-to Sections: Include a sub-menu that allows users to jump to specific sections like 'Details', 'Itinerary', or 'Reviews'. This enhances user experience, especially on lengthy pages.

Website conclusions

The perfect tour page is a blend of clear information, trust-building elements, and user-friendly design. It should not only provide comprehensive details about the tour but also guide visitors smoothly towards making a booking. The ultimate goal is to convert interest into revenue, and this is the approach we also took for Mr. & Mrs. Egypt.

 Check out the resource section for specific videos on my ultimate guide for not only a tour page, but a home page too.

Getting to know Mr & Mrs Egypt customer and competitors

Understanding the ideal customer for Mr & Mrs Egypt is crucial. By pinpointing exactly who you're marketing to, you can tailor your strategies, sales approaches, and communication to better resonate with them.

In the Workshop, they defined their target customer profile as follows:

Location: US or Western Europe
Age Range: 40-60+
Income: Disposable income available
Interests: Egypt, History, Archaeology

This is their current perception of their customer base. Initially, Carol had thought the target audience included individuals in their early 20s and older. To ensure we accurately reach the right demographic, we need to delve deeper through research, leveraging both online tools and official data sources.

I'll be using the following methods and tools to gather comprehensive insights and refine the target audience, ensuring our marketing efforts are focused on the most relevant customer segments.

Exploring travel reports

When it comes to understanding who's travelling to a destination like Egypt, the first port of call should always be data from reliable sources, such as government agencies and independent bodies. These entities compile comprehensive reports on traveller behaviour, demographics, and trends, providing invaluable insights into potential markets.

There are several places where you can find this information:

- Destination Marketing Organizations (DMOs)
- Statista
- Report Linker
- Nielsen
- IBISWorld
- World Travel & Tourism Council (WTTC)**

Now, it's worth noting that some of these reports might sit behind a paywall. While it can be tempting to bypass them, investing in a detailed report might be in your best interest, especially if it provides critical data that could influence your marketing strategy.

I began with a straightforward Google search: *"Traveller numbers to Egypt 2023."*

The first article that caught my eye was from TravelWorld.com, which reported:

"Egypt receives a record 15 million tourists in 2023. The total number of tourists visiting Egypt during the first four months of 2024 increased by 27 percent, supported by inbound tourism from Arab countries, which witnessed a 54 percent growth compared to the same period in 2023."

This nugget of information reveals a few key points. First, tourism in Egypt saw a significant uptick in 2023, with continued growth into 2024. Importantly, the majority of this surge was driven by visitors from Arab countries, indicating a shift in Egypt's tourism dynamics. While this could signal an opportunity for Mr & Mrs Egypt to tap into this growing market, it may not align perfectly with their current focus.

Carol, the face of Mr & Mrs Egypt, appeals primarily to Western tourists—her background and approach resonate more with these travellers than with those from Arab nations. However, this doesn't mean the latter group should be dismissed. If Atef were to shift focus, targeting Arab tourists could be a viable strategy. It's all about understanding the market and adapting accordingly.

During the same search, I stumbled upon two travel reports, one from the World Travel & Tourism Council (WTTC), and another from Statista. Although access to these required payment. I decided to purchase the report from Statista as it provides some vital information.

The data shed light on the steady growth of US travellers to Egypt over recent years. For instance, the number of American tourists visiting Egypt rose from 240,000 in 2013 to 358,000 in 2017, reflecting an increase of approximately 30,000 US tourists each year.

However, one of the most striking statistics comes from 2022, when the number of American tourists arriving in Egypt surged to 676,000—more than double the 322,000 from the previous year (Covid years!). This significant increase highlights a growing interest among US travellers in exploring Egypt, underscoring the potential market Mr & Mrs Egypt could tap into. This data is not only encouraging but also offers a solid foundation on which to build targeted marketing strategies aimed at attracting these high-potential visitors.

Moreover, the report highlighted a similar trend among UK residents. The number of visits from the United Kingdom to Egypt saw a significant rise in 2022, bouncing back to 267,000 after plummeting to just 59,000 in 2021 due to the COVID-19 pandemic. This rebound indicates a renewed interest in Egypt among British travellers, presenting another lucrative market opportunity for Mr & Mrs Egypt to explore.

Some of you might consider these visitor numbers modest, but for Mr & Mrs Egypt, this is perfectly in line with their business model. They specialise in offering bespoke, custom experiences, catering to a select group of travellers each year. As a boutique operator, they don't rely on high volumes, so these market figures are more than sufficient for their needs.

Harnessing AI to gather strategic insights

Another valuable resource in this digital age is AI tools like ChatGPT. These tools can swiftly pull together data and point you toward credible sources. For example, I asked ChatGPT:

"Can you source how many US travellers visited Egypt in 2023? I am also looking for demographic information like age and gender."

ChatGPT guided me to the U.S. government's trade site, trade.gov, where I found downloadable reports and spreadsheets filled with inbound and outbound travel data. After sifting through an extensive document, I uncovered some interesting statistics for all outbound travel:

- **Travel Companions:** 23.9% of travellers went with a partner, and 90% of these didn't bring children. Meanwhile, 60.3% travelled alone.
- **Purpose of Travel:** 58.9% were on vacation, while 28.8% visited friends and family.
- **Length of Stay:** Travellers spent varying amounts of time abroad, with 27.0% staying 4-7 nights, 19.3% for 8-10 nights, and 17.8% for 11-14 nights.
- **Popular Departure Airports:** Miami, Atlanta, New Jersey, and New York were the most common departure points.
- **Activities Engaged:** Shopping and sightseeing topped the list, with 72.7% shopping and 81.3% sightseeing. Other activities included visiting historical locations (43.0%), experiencing fine dining (37.4%), and attending cultural or ethnic heritage sites (32.7%).

From these statistics, we learn that travellers are diverse in their interests and travel habits. However, only 0.6% of the travellers in this data set above visited Egypt. This percentage might seem small, but as stated earlier, it still provides a critical insight into the niche market Mr & Mrs Egypt could be targeting. Understanding who these travellers are—their interests, spending habits, and travel patterns—can help fine-tune the marketing strategy to attract more of them.

Use Google Trends for up-to-date search data

Another powerful tool that can offer valuable insights for Mr & Mrs Egypt is Google Trends. By analysing the popularity of search terms over time, Google Trends enables us to gauge interest in specific destinations, experiences, and travel-related topics. For a boutique operator like Mr & Mrs Egypt, understanding what potential travellers are searching for can be incredibly beneficial in tailoring their offerings to meet current demands.

This platform provides real-time data on search trends across different regions, helping them identify when and where interest in Egypt peaks. For instance, if there's a surge in searches for "Egyptian cultural tours" or "Nile cruises" at a particular time of year, Mr & Mrs Egypt can align their marketing efforts accordingly, ensuring they reach their target audience at the right moment. Additionally, Google Trends can help them compare the popularity of different search terms, allowing them to focus on the experiences that resonate most with their potential customers.

In essence, Google Trends offers a window into the minds of travellers, enabling Mr & Mrs Egypt to stay ahead of the curve and strategically position themselves in the market.

Looking over the data for the last 12 months, I can see an average of 54 searches per week in the US for 'Trip to Egypt'. Google Trends also tells me that the top 10 popular states for these searches are New Mexico, New Jersey, Virginia, Georgia, Oklahoma, Pennsylvania, New York, Illinois, Oregon and Wisconsin.

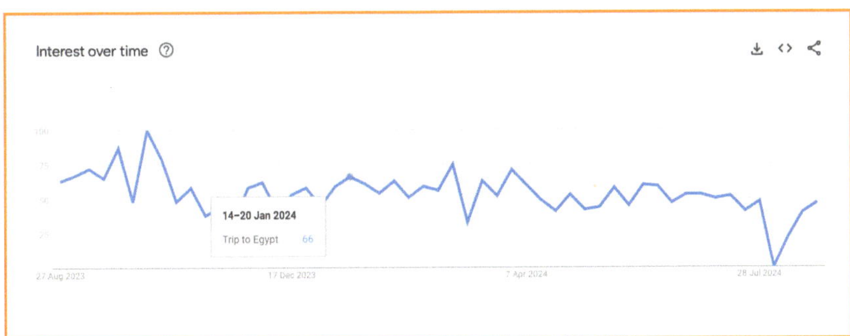

When using the term 'Visit Egypt', again the average is around 54 searches per week, but this time the most popular destinations are, District of Columbia, Vermont, New Hampshire, California, New Jersey, Washington, Georgia, Hawaii, New York and Idaho. The term 'Things to do in Egypt' also found similar stats.

If these are the most popular areas in the US that are searching for Trips to Egypt, then it makes sense that these are added to the mix when creating the likes of targeted ad campaigns.

Maximising market insights with AirDNA

Another highly valuable tool, yet often underutilised, is AirDNA. This platform is well worth the monthly subscription, as it provides crucial data on aspects like occupancy rates and length of stay. Such insights are not only essential for understanding the types of customers who might be visiting your destination from a marketing perspective, but they also help you tailor your own products to meet market demands.

For instance, if the data shows that the average stay in a destination is three days, offering a 14-day experience might significantly limit your booking potential. By aligning your offerings with the typical length of stay, you increase your chances of attracting the right customers.

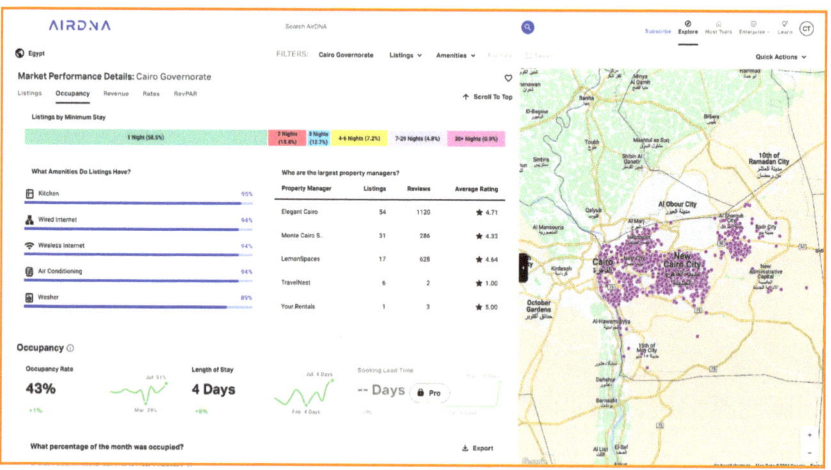

When we examine the data for a popular destination like Cairo, we can see that, at the time of writing, the occupancy rate is 43%. Although this is relatively low, it is an improvement of one percent compared to the previous 12 months. Additionally, the average stay is four days (three nights), with 82% of bookings for entire homes and 17% for private rooms, indicating both individual and group travel preferences.

Interestingly, despite the average stay being four days, 4.8% of all rentals cater to those staying between 7 and 29 days. This suggests that there is still a substantial market for longer experiences, which could be an opportunity for operators like Mr & Mrs Egypt.

Moreover, AirDNA's mapping feature is particularly insightful. It shows clusters of properties where potential customers of Mr & Mrs Egypt might be staying. While this information might be less relevant for multi-day tour operators, it is incredibly useful for day tour providers. They can use this data to strategically target Facebook ads in these high-density areas, ensuring their marketing efforts reach the right audience.

All these insights collectively help in better understanding and refining Mr & Mrs Egypt's target audience, allowing for more informed and effective business decisions.

Maximise marketing impact with direct flight information

Understanding which US states offer direct flights to Cairo can be a game-changer for Mr & Mrs Egypt's marketing strategy. By knowing these routes, you can precisely target potential travellers who have the most convenient access to your bespoke experiences in Egypt.

A quick search for "which US airports fly direct to Cairo?" reveals that John F. Kennedy International Airport in New York and Washington Dulles International Airport are major gateways.

This information is invaluable not only for pinpointing primary target markets but also for identifying neighbouring states where travellers might be willing to make a short journey to access a direct flight.

For Mr & Mrs Egypt, this means you can create focused marketing campaigns that appeal directly to consumers in these regions. By highlighting the ease of direct flights to Cairo and the unique, custom experiences you offer, you can more effectively capture the interest of travellers already inclined to visit Egypt.

Moreover, understanding flight paths allows you to time your marketing efforts strategically, aligning them with peak travel seasons or promotional periods. Consider geo-targeted ads that specifically reach audiences in and around these key states, showcasing how effortless it is to embark on a journey to Egypt with Mr & Mrs Egypt.

Unlocking audience insights with Google Analytics

Another invaluable tool at Mr & Mrs Egypt's disposal is Google Analytics. This platform offers a wealth of data that can help refine and pinpoint your target demographics. By analysing metrics such as user age, gender, location, and interests, you can gain a clearer picture of who is actually visiting your website and engaging with your content. This information is crucial in tailoring your offerings and marketing strategies to better align with the audience that is most likely to convert into customers.

For instance, if Google Analytics reveals that a significant portion of your website visitors are within a particular age group or geographical area, you can adjust your marketing efforts to focus more heavily on these demographics. This might involve creating targeted ad campaigns, developing content that resonates with these specific groups, or even tweaking your product offerings to better meet their needs.

If all your marketing materials feature photography of individuals in their 20s and 30s, but your target audience is 50 and older, your messaging is unlikely to resonate with the people you're trying to reach. This mismatch can dilute the effectiveness of your marketing efforts, making it harder to connect with your intended audience.

However, Google Analytics doesn't just show you who is interested in your business; it can also highlight potential disconnects between your intended audience and the one you're actually reaching. If the data reveals that your site is attracting visitors who don't match your ideal customer profile, it could be a sign that your current marketing efforts are not resonating with the right audience.

For example, if Mr & Mrs Egypt aims to attract high-income travellers from the US and Europe, but the majority of their traffic comes from younger, budget-conscious travellers from different regions, it may indicate a misalignment in their messaging or ad targeting. This disconnect could mean that your current marketing is failing to speak to the audience you truly want to attract.

By delving into Mr & Mrs Egypt's Google Analytics, we gain

valuable insights into their current audience demographics. The data reveals that the United States is indeed the leading source of visitors to their website, with the United Kingdom trailing behind in second place. Gender distribution is fairly balanced, with 51.3% of visitors being female and 48.7% male.

The top five interests among these visitors are particularly telling:

- Travel/Travel Buffs
- Technology/Technophiles
- Lifestyles & Hobbies/Shutterbugs
- News & Politics/Avid News Readers
- Travel/Travel Buffs/Beachbound Travelers

These interests provide a clear direction for ad targeting, enabling Mr & Mrs Egypt to craft campaigns that speak directly to these specific groups.

However, there's an intriguing aspect to the age demographics. The primary age range visiting the site is 18-34, with 35-54 following closely behind. Notably, the 45-54 age group is the most engaged on the site. This engagement suggests that those aged 45-54 are genuinely interested in experiencing Egypt, while the younger audience may largely consist of students researching Egyptian history or those seeking budget travel options.

This disparity highlights a potential disconnect in the current marketing strategy. While the aim is to attract an older, more affluent demographic, the data indicates that the messaging may be resonating more with a younger audience. This could suggest that Mr & Mrs Egypt's marketing is not yet fully aligned with their target market of older, more experience-focused travellers.

Adjusting the focus to better cater to the 45-54 age group—perhaps by refining the imagery, content, and messaging to reflect their preferences—could help bridge this gap and more effectively attract the desired audience.

Engaging existing customers

In addition to gathering insights from potential customers, it's equally important to engage with your existing and past customers to understand their experiences and perceptions of Mr & Mrs Egypt. Conducting a short survey targeted at these individuals can provide valuable feedback that helps refine your customer personas and better inform your marketing strategies.

To encourage more survey submissions and increase participation, consider running a competition where respondents have the chance to win a gift certificate towards a future tour or experience with your business. This incentive can significantly boost response rates, as it offers a tangible reward for taking the time to provide feedback. By offering a prize that directly relates to your services, you not only gather valuable insights but also keep your brand top of mind for those who may be considering another trip to Egypt. This approach not only enriches your data collection but also strengthens customer engagement and loyalty.

Using tools like SurveyMonkey, Typeform, Google Sheets or Pollfish can help reveal key insights into who they are, what they value, and how they perceive your brand. By asking questions about their experiences, preferences, and demographics, you can identify patterns and trends that may not be apparent through other means.

For example, you might discover that a significant portion of your customers falls within a particular age group or shares common interests. This information can help you refine your customer personas, ensuring that they more accurately reflect your actual customer base.

Furthermore, understanding your customers' pain points or areas where they see room for improvement can inform future marketing efforts, product development, and customer service strategies. By aligning your offerings more closely with the needs and desires of your current customers, you can enhance customer satisfaction, increase repeat business, and attract new customers who fit your ideal profile.

For Mr & Mrs Egypt, we used Pollfish but I will cover this a little later.

Crafting Mr & Mrs Egypt's customer persona(s)

Now that we have a mountain of data on potential customers, we can begin crafting detailed customer personas to effectively target with our marketing efforts. These personas will serve as the foundation for developing a focused and strategic marketing approach, ensuring that every aspect of Mr & Mrs Egypt's business resonates with the right audience. By aligning their offerings with the specific needs and desires of these personas, we can optimise our chances of attracting and engaging the ideal customers.

Here are some personas we created following the research...

Persona 1: The Affluent Explorer

Name: Susan Walker
Age: 52
Location: USA
Occupation: Senior Executive at a Financial Services Firm
Income: $200,000+ annually
Marital Status: Married, with adult children
Education: Master's Degree
Interests: Cultural heritage, history, fine dining, luxury travel experiences
Travel Habits: Travels internationally 2-3 times a year, often to culturally rich destinations; prefers bespoke, high-end tours
Motivations: Seeks meaningful travel experiences that offer deep cultural immersion and a touch of luxury. Values exclusivity and personalised services.

Why This Persona?

Susan represents the ideal customer for Mr & Mrs Egypt—a discerning traveller who appreciates the unique blend of luxury and cultural richness that Egypt offers. Her interest in history and cultural heritage aligns perfectly with the experiences Mr &

Mrs Egypt provides, such as private tours of the Pyramids, Nile cruises, and exclusive visits to ancient temples. As someone with a high disposable income, Susan is willing to invest in premium travel experiences that offer comfort, exclusivity, and a deeper understanding of the places she visits.

Persona 2: The Cultural Enthusiast

Name: Mark Johnson
Age: 45
Location: USA
Occupation: University Professor of History
Income: $150,000 annually
Marital Status: Married, with one teenage child
Education: PhD in History
Interests: Archaeology, ancient civilizations, educational travel, photography
Travel Habits: Travels internationally once a year, primarily to destinations with historical significance; prefers well-structured tours that offer in-depth learning opportunities
Motivations: Desires to explore the world's historical sites with expert guidance. Values educational content and the chance to engage with local experts and historians.

Why This Persona?

Mark represents a key demographic that is deeply interested in the educational and historical aspects of travel. His passion for archaeology and ancient civilisations makes him a prime candidate for the unique, informative tours offered by Mr & Mrs

Egypt. Mark's preference for structured, educational travel aligns well with the company's ability to provide expert-led tours that delve into the rich history and culture of Egypt. Additionally, his academic background and interest in photography suggest that he would appreciate and share the in-depth experiences offered by Mr & Mrs Egypt, potentially becoming a long-term advocate for the brand.

Persona 3: The Solo Adventurer

Name: Emily Parker
Age: 40
Location: USA
Occupation: Freelance Writer and Travel Blogger
Income: $85,000 annually
Marital Status: Single
Education: Bachelor's Degree
Interests: Solo travel, off-the-beaten-path destinations, cultural immersion, sustainable tourism
Travel Habits: Travels frequently, often several times a year, with a preference for solo trips to unique, culturally rich locations
Motivations: Seeks authentic, immersive travel experiences that allow for personal growth and adventure. Values sustainability, local interactions, and experiences that go beyond typical tourist attractions.

Why This Persona?

Emily represents a growing demographic of solo travellers who prioritise cultural immersion and unique experiences over traditional tourist routes. As someone who travels frequently and prefers destinations that offer authenticity and depth, she is the perfect candidate for Mr & Mrs Egypt's bespoke tours. Her interest in sustainable tourism and off-the-beaten-path experiences aligns well with the company's ability to provide intimate, locally-driven tours that showcase Egypt's hidden gems. Emily's influence as a travel blogger also makes her a valuable advocate, as she is likely to share her experiences with a broad audience, amplifying Mr & Mrs Egypt's reach.

This persona is crucial for tapping into the solo travel market—a segment that continues to grow as more individuals seek independent and transformative travel experiences (Remember, according to Trade.gov, 60.3% travelled alone). By catering to this group, Mr & Mrs Egypt can expand their appeal and attract a clientele that values depth, authenticity, and personal adventure.

Final thoughts on personas

Although the focus of the personas above is on the US market, these profiles are equally applicable to the UK market. The underlying motivations, interests, and behaviours of affluent travellers seeking cultural immersion, luxury experiences, and unique adventures are consistent across both regions.

However, to streamline our marketing efforts and maintain a clear focus, we will concentrate exclusively on the US market for the time being.

Gather insights with a consumer survey

Now that we have identified the persona Mr & Mrs Egypt aims to target, the final piece of the puzzle is to engage this demographic directly. By asking them a series of carefully crafted questions, we can ensure that what Mr & Mrs Egypt offers aligns with the desires and expectations of their target audience.

To conduct this survey, we utilised the research tool Pollfish to design the survey, target our specific audience, and collect the data. Pollfish operates on a pay-per-survey model and, while it isn't a free service, the investment is worthwhile. The minimum cost for a survey is around USD $800, which may seem significant, but the insights gained are invaluable and can make a substantial difference in ensuring that your offerings align with the needs and desires of your target market.

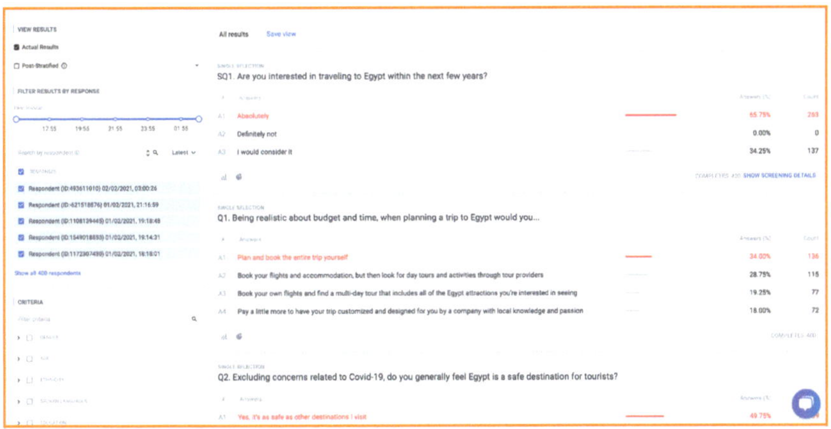

We engaged with 400 respondents who were at least considering, if not actively interested in, travelling to Egypt in the near future. These initial screening questions were vital to ensure that the insights gathered were relevant and applicable.

Additionally, Pollfish offers the flexibility to distribute your survey not only to a targeted audience but also to your existing customers. This feature allows you to gather insights directly from those who are already familiar with your brand, providing a deeper understanding of their preferences and expectations.

The survey revealed several key insights into the demographics, preferences, and concerns of these potential travellers. Notably, the majority of respondents fell within the 35-44 age range (65%), with a significant portion earning over $150,000 annually. This aligns well with the luxury market that Mr & Mrs Egypt aims to target. Additionally, 75% of respondents were married, and 85% held a university or post-graduate degree, further indicating a well-educated, affluent demographic.

Safety perceptions were also explored, with 50% of respondents believing that Egypt is as safe as other destinations they visit, and only a small fraction (3.25%) viewing it as dangerous. This is encouraging for Mr & Mrs Egypt, as it suggests that safety concerns are not a major barrier for most potential customers. Especially important for the female travellers.

When it comes to travel preferences, the survey highlighted that while 34% of respondents prefer to plan and book their entire trip themselves, 49% would seek out day or multi-day tours after booking their own flights. Interestingly, among the 45-54 age group, 33% indicated they would pay more for a fully customised tour. This suggests a promising market for Mr & Mrs Egypt to offer tailored, high-end experiences.

The survey also delved into the top attractions and activities of interest. Luxor, the Pyramids of Giza, and a Nile River cruise were among the most popular choices, with over 69% of respondents expressing interest in these iconic sites. On the other hand, less well-known destinations like the Abu Simbel Temples garnered lower interest, highlighting an opportunity for Mr & Mrs Egypt to educate potential travellers about these lesser-known gems.

Finally, the survey explored price expectations for a 10-day customised trip. Most respondents (68%) expected such a holiday to cost between $2,000 and $4,000, with those in the 45-54 age range more likely to anticipate costs on the lower end of that spectrum. This insight is invaluable for setting pricing strategies that align with customer expectations while maintaining the perceived value of a luxury experience.

Overall, the insights from this consumer survey provide a solid foundation for Mr & Mrs Egypt to refine their target audience, tailor their offerings, and optimise their marketing strategies to resonate with the right demographic. By aligning their services with the preferences and expectations of potential customers, they can position themselves effectively in the competitive luxury travel market to Egypt.

Conducting a competitor analysis

In the final stage of research for Mr & Mrs Egypt, we'll dive deeply into their competitors to evaluate tours, content, current ads, brand positioning, unique selling propositions (USPs), and other factors that could impact Carol and Atef's business, both positively and negatively.

Understanding how competitors position themselves in the market, their branding strategies, and their SEO goals is extremely valuable. By analysing what competitors do well and identifying their mistakes—such as poorly executed website features or ineffective marketing activities—you can gain insights that help Mr & Mrs Egypt excel.

Although a comprehensive SEO competitor analysis is challenging at this stage due to the evolving nature of Mr & Mrs Egypt's products and website, we can still gather valuable information. This involves reviewing competitors' websites to note strengths and weaknesses, which will inform Mr & Mrs Egypt's digital strategy.

To respect the confidentiality of these businesses, I won't reveal the competitors directly here. Instead, I'll just provide an overview and call them Competitor One and so on...

Competitor One: displays a strong SEO presence, ranking well for various keywords, though their content is often poorly integrated with obvious keyword stuffing. Their imagery is largely generic stock photos, lacking originality and a personal touch. While their product range is extensive, it lacks customisation options, and their website suffers from low-quality visuals and a somewhat uninspired user experience.

Competitor Two: offers a vast array of products and services, but their website is sparse on content, making it difficult for users to gauge the brand's personality. The user journey is convoluted, with too many clicks required to reach product details. The site also lacks any obvious attempt to address safety concerns, which could deter potential customers. Additionally, they have no visible reviews, which is a significant oversight given the importance of social proof in the travel industry.

Competitor Three: emphasises SEO, often at the expense of readability and user engagement. While they do rank well for important keywords, their content can be off-putting due to its overt optimisation. The website features a mix of high and low-quality images, many of which feel impersonal. Their product offerings are somewhat confusing, with unclear distinctions between different tour categories. However, they do have a dedicated reviews section, which is well-executed and linked to external platforms like TripAdvisor, providing credibility.

Overall, while each competitor has its strengths, there are clear areas where Mr & Mrs Egypt can excel, such as by providing more personalised and engaging content, simplifying the user journey, and leveraging authentic, high-quality imagery to stand out in the market.

Step-by-step guide to conducting a competitor analysis

Conducting a thorough competitor analysis is crucial for understanding your position in the market and identifying opportunities for growth. By systematically examining your competitors' strategies, strengths, and weaknesses, you can uncover insights that will help you refine your own business approach.

Below, I will walk you through a step-by-step process for analysing your competitors, from identifying who they are to using the findings to shape your own strategic decisions.

Step 1: Identifying competitors

Direct competitors

The first step in any competitor analysis is to clearly identify who your direct competitors are. These are the businesses offering similar products or services that target the same customer base as you. Direct competitors are often the most obvious threats because they are vying for the same market share. Identifying them involves researching companies that operate within your industry, offer similar value propositions, and appeal to the same demographic.

You can start by searching online, looking at industry reports, or even asking customers which other companies they considered before choosing yours. Understanding who your direct competitors are will allow you to focus your analysis on the most relevant players in your market, providing insights into how you can differentiate yourself and gain a competitive edge.

Indirect competitors

While direct competitors are easy to spot, it's equally important to consider indirect competitors—those businesses offering different products or services that could serve as alternatives to what you offer. These competitors may not appear to be a direct threat at first glance, but they can capture market share by meeting the same customer needs in a different way.

For example, if you run a tour company, an indirect competitor could be a travel guidebook or a DIY travel planning app. Identifying these indirect competitors requires thinking more broadly about your customers' needs and the various ways they might choose to fulfill them. By understanding the full landscape of competition, including indirect competitors, you can better position your business to offer something unique that captures customers' attention.

Tools for identifying competitors

To identify both direct and indirect competitors effectively, there are several tools and methods you can use. Online searches and industry directories are a good starting point for discovering companies that operate within your niche. Tools like Google Alerts can notify you whenever a competitor is mentioned online, while platforms like LinkedIn can help you identify competitors by exploring the connections of your current B2B clients and partners.

Additionally, market research tools such as SEMrush, Ahrefs, or Moz can provide valuable insights into who is competing for the same keywords and online visibility. Social media platforms also offer a wealth of information about competitors, as you can observe their engagement with followers, the content they post, and how they interact with their audience.

By leveraging these tools, you can compile a comprehensive list of competitors to analyse, ensuring that your strategy is informed by a full understanding of the competitive landscape.

Step 2: Research competitor products and services

Understanding what your competitors offer is a crucial part of any competitor analysis. This step involves a deep dive into their product and service offerings to uncover what makes them stand out and how they compare to your own. By examining the specifics of what your competitors bring to the table, you can better position your products and services in the market, identify potential gaps, and discover new opportunities for differentiation.

Product/service offerings

Begin by compiling a detailed overview of the products and services your competitors provide. This includes not only the range of products or tours they offer but also any unique features or benefits they highlight. Look at how they present these offerings on their websites—what categories do they use, how do they describe each product, and what kind of imagery or videos do they use to sell them? This information will give you insights into their positioning and help you understand what aspects of their offerings appeal most to customers.

To make this process easier, I've developed a handy Chrome plugin specifically designed for gathering information on competitor products and services. This tool allows you to select the title, URL, and price from a list of products or tours on any site and automatically downloads this data into a spreadsheet.

Additionally, the spreadsheet will calculate the average tour price from the list, giving you a clear picture of how your competitors price their offerings. You can download this tool for free from the Chrome Store by searching for "TMA Product Research."

Pricing strategies

Once you've gathered detailed information on your competitors' products and services, the next step is to analyse their pricing strategies. Understanding how your competitors price their offerings can provide valuable insights into their market positioning, target audience, and perceived value. Are they positioned as a budget option, mid-range, or premium service? Do they use dynamic pricing, discounts, or package deals to attract customers?

With the data collected using the Chrome plugin, you can easily compare prices across different competitors and see where your pricing fits in. The average tour price calculation feature in the spreadsheet allows you to quickly assess the overall pricing landscape. This comparison will help you determine whether your pricing strategy is competitive and whether there's room to adjust your prices to better align with your target market.

By thoroughly researching your competitors' products, services, and pricing, you can identify areas where you can innovate, improve, or differentiate your offerings. This step lays the groundwork for making strategic decisions about how to position your products and services in the market, ensuring that you stay competitive and continue to attract your ideal customers.

Step 3: Analyse competitor platforms and content

This step involves a comprehensive review of each competitor's digital presence, content marketing efforts, social media activity, and advertising campaigns.

Website analysis

Your competitors' websites are often the first point of contact for potential customers, making them a key focus in your analysis. Start by evaluating the overall design and user experience (UX) of their websites. Is the site visually appealing? Is it easy to navigate? Pay attention to the structure, the quality of the content, and the calls to action.

Next, assess their SEO practices. Tools like SEMrush or Ahrefs can help you analyse how well their sites are optimised for search engines. Look at the keywords they're targeting, the quality of their meta tags, and the effectiveness of their internal linking strategy. This will give you insight into how they attract organic traffic and rank in search engine results.

Social media presence

Analysing your competitors' social media presence can provide valuable insights into their audience engagement, content strategy, and overall brand voice. Start by identifying the platforms they are most active on—Facebook, Instagram, Twitter, LinkedIn, or perhaps niche platforms like Pinterest or TikTok.

Evaluate the frequency and quality of their posts. Are they posting regularly? What types of content are they sharing—blog posts, videos, user-generated content, or promotional offers? Also, look at their engagement metrics: likes, shares, comments, and followers. High engagement levels often indicate a strong connection with their audience. Tools like Social Pilot or Social Blade can help you track and compare these metrics.

Content marketing

Start by reviewing the types of content they produce—blog posts, articles, videos, infographics, or podcasts. Is their content informative and engaging? Does it address the pain points of their audience?

Examine how they distribute their content. Are they leveraging their blog, email newsletters, or third-party platforms? Also, consider the quality and frequency of their content updates. A regular content schedule suggests a well-planned strategy, while infrequent or low-quality content can indicate a lack of focus. Tools like BuzzSumo can help you identify the most shared content and topics in your industry, providing inspiration for your own content marketing efforts.

Advertising campaigns

Start by identifying the platforms they use for advertising—Google Ads, Facebook Ads, Instagram, or LinkedIn. Are they investing in paid search, display ads, or social media advertising? Tools like SpyFu or AdBeat can provide insights into their ad spending, the keywords they're bidding on, and the overall structure of their campaigns.

Pay attention to the messaging and design of their ads. Are they using compelling visuals, strong calls to action, or promotional offers? Analyse the consistency of their messaging across different ad platforms. Consistency often indicates a well-coordinated marketing effort, which is key to reinforcing brand identity.

In summary, analysing your competitors' marketing strategies provides a comprehensive view of their strengths and weaknesses.

Step 4: Evaluate customer experience

This step involves analysing customer reviews, testing customer support, and assessing the overall user experience on your competitors' platforms.

Customer reviews and testimonials

Start by exploring reviews on platforms like Google, TripAdvisor, Yelp, and social media. Pay close attention to both positive and negative feedback—what are customers praising, and what are the common complaints? Look for patterns in the reviews, such as consistent praise for a particular service or repeated issues with customer service.

Testimonials on competitor websites can also reveal how they highlight their strengths. Do they feature reviews prominently? Are the testimonials specific and detailed, or are they generic? This information can help you understand the aspects of the customer experience that matter most to your shared audience.

To help collate reviews on platforms like Google or Facebook, you can use a handy tool called Export Comments (exportcomments. com) to do this for you.

Customer support

Reach out to their customer service channels—whether through email, phone, live chat, or social media—and assess the quality of the interaction. How quickly do they respond? Is the service professional and helpful? Do they go above and beyond to assist you, or is the response lacklustre? Have a friend, or yourself, to take one of their tours and see how they communicate.

Step 5: Analyse competitor brand presence

This step involves analysing how your competitors position their brand, the visual identity they project, and their media presence.

Brand Positioning

To analyse your competitors' brand positioning, start by examining their mission statements, taglines, and key messaging across various platforms. Are they positioning themselves as luxury providers, budget-friendly options, or experts in a specific niche? Look at how they communicate their value propositions—what promises are they making to their customers, and how do they differentiate themselves from others in the market?

Consider how consistently they maintain this positioning across all customer touchpoints, including their website, social media, and marketing materials. Consistent and clear brand positioning can build strong brand equity and make a company more memorable.

Visual Identity

Your competitors' visual identity is the first impression they make on potential customers, and it should reflect their brand's values and personality. Start by analysing their logo design. Is it modern, traditional, playful, or serious? How does it align with the type of service they offer and the audience they are targeting?

Next, examine their use of colour and typography. Are their colour choices consistent across all platforms, and do they evoke the right emotions for their brand? For example, a luxury tour operator might use a sophisticated palette of deep blues and golds, while an adventure travel company might opt for bold, vibrant colours. Consistency in visual identity is key to building brand recognition.

Public Relations

Analysing your competitors' PR efforts can provide insights into how they manage their reputation and engage with the public. Start by researching their presence in the media—are they frequently featured in travel publications, news articles, or online blogs? What kind of stories are being told about them, and how do these stories align with their brand positioning?

Look at how they handle public relations crises, if any have occurred. Did they respond quickly and effectively? A brand's ability to manage negative publicity can significantly impact customer trust and loyalty. Additionally, consider their proactive PR efforts, such as press releases, sponsorships, or participation in industry events. These activities can enhance their credibility and visibility in the market.

By thoroughly examining their brand positioning, visual identity, and public relations efforts, you can identify ways to strengthen your own brand and create a distinct, memorable identity that resonates with your target audience.

Step 6: assess competitor strengths and weaknesses (SWOT)

By identifying where your competitors excel and where they fall short, you can uncover opportunities to differentiate your brand, exploit market gaps, and avoid their pitfalls. This step involves conducting a SWOT (Strengths, Weaknesses, Opportunities, and Threats) analysis for each competitor, identifying potential opportunities for your business, and recognising threats posed by their strengths.

Start by listing each competitor's strengths—these could include brand reputation, customer loyalty, innovative products, or strong online presence. For example, if a competitor has a highly engaged social media following, this is a strength that could indicate their brand resonates well with their audience.

Strengths

1. **Unique Experiences:** Mr & Mrs Egypt offer highly personalised, bespoke tours that cater to the individual preferences of each customer, setting them apart from competitors who provide more standardised packages.
2. **Extensive Experience:** Atef has over 33 years of experience in the tourism industry, with a deep knowledge of Egypt and strong local connections, allowing access to places that other operators cannot offer.
3. **Focus on Safety and Security:** Carol places great emphasis on ensuring the safety and security of Western European and North American tourists, including the use of fully licensed Egyptologist guides.
4. **24/7 Availability:** The company is dedicated to customer service, with Atef personally addressing any issues that may arise during the tours, ensuring a high level of care and flexibility.
5. **Cultural Expertise:** The combination of Carol's and Atef's knowledge of Egypt's history and culture appeals to a broad audience.
6. **Multilingual and International Focus:** Carol's understanding of Western tourist needs enhances the company's appeal to English-speaking travellers.

Weaknesses

1. **Limited Brand Awareness:** Despite their strong offering, Mr & Mrs Egypt may suffer from a lack of brand visibility in a competitive market of Egyptian tour operators.
2. **Outdated Digital Presence:** The company's website is noted as being outdated, which may negatively impact the user experience and initial perceptions from potential customers.
3. **Small Team:** The business is heavily reliant on Carol and Atef for day-to-day operations, which could become a limitation as the company grows, particularly during busy periods.
4. **Price Perception:** Competing against cheaper, unlicensed operators may make it difficult to justify higher prices, even though these competitors may offer lower-quality or less secure experiences.

Opportunities

1. **Growing Demand for Authentic Experiences:** There is increasing demand for personalised and authentic travel experiences, which Mr & Mrs Egypt can capitalise on with their bespoke tour offerings.
2. **Digital Marketing:** By improving their website and investing in SEO, social media, and digital advertising (e.g. Google Ads), they could significantly increase visibility and attract direct bookings from international customers.
3. **Partnerships and Referrals:** Forming partnerships with international travel agencies, influencers, and travel bloggers could help expand their reach and drive more bookings.
4. **Referral and Review Strategies:** Encouraging satisfied customers to leave reviews on platforms like TripAdvisor and Google, alongside a referral programme, could drive growth through word-of-mouth and positive online presence.

Threats

1. **Political and Economic Instability:** Like all tourism businesses in Egypt, external factors such as political instability or global economic downturns could negatively affect tourism demand.
2. **Competition from Unlicensed Operators:** Competing with lower-cost, unlicensed operators who may not follow regulations could make it harder to justify their higher prices, especially for budget-conscious travellers.
3. **Shifting Consumer Preferences:** If consumers increasingly opt for cheaper, standardised tours offered by large travel agencies or online travel agencies (OTAs), Mr & Mrs Egypt may struggle to maintain their niche appeal.
4. **Over-reliance on Key Personnel:** With Carol and Atef being central to the business, any personal issues, health problems, or burnout could significantly affect the company's ability to deliver services effectively.

Next, identify their weaknesses—areas where they may be underperforming. This could be anything from poor customer service, limited product range, outdated technology, or a lack of innovation. Weaknesses are often opportunities in disguise; if you can address these gaps in your own business, you can gain a competitive advantage. A competitor's slow response time to customer inquiries, for instance, might present an opportunity for you to shine by offering superior customer service.

Assessing opportunities involves looking for market trends or unmet needs that your competitors are not fully capitalising on. This could be a new demographic that is emerging, changes in consumer behaviour, or advances in technology that your business could leverage.

Finally, consider the threats posed by your competitors' strengths. A well-established competitor with a loyal customer base, for example, could make it challenging for your business to gain market share.

Step 7: Monitor competitor activity

This final step involves setting up ongoing surveillance to track your competitors' movements and regularly updating your analysis to reflect the latest developments.

Ongoing surveillance of your competitors involves systematically tracking their activities across various platforms and channels. This can include monitoring their website updates, new product launches, pricing changes, marketing campaigns, and social media activity. Tools like Google Alerts can notify you whenever your competitors are mentioned online, allowing you to stay informed about their latest moves. Additionally, platforms like Mention and Brand24 offer more comprehensive monitoring of brand mentions across the web and social media.

Subscribing to your competitors' newsletters and following their social media accounts can also provide valuable insights. This allows you to see how they communicate with their audience, what promotions they're running, and how they engage with their customers. Pay attention to any changes in their messaging, the introduction of new products or services, and the timing of their campaigns.

Conclusions on knowing your customer and competitors

By conducting thorough research—whether through government reports, AI and online tools, or consumer surveys—you can gather the necessary data to make informed decisions.

Understanding who your customers are, what they value, and how they interact with your brand is crucial to crafting marketing strategies that resonate. Moreover, insights gained from platforms like Google Analytics can help identify any disconnects between your intended audience and those you're currently reaching, allowing for timely adjustments.

Engaging with both potential and existing customers through targeted surveys provides deeper insight into their preferences and expectations, enabling Mr & Mrs Egypt to fine-tune their offerings and marketing efforts. The data reveals not only who your customers are but also how to better serve them, ensuring that your services align with their needs and desires.

As you continue to refine your customer personas and strategies, remember that all this research is not a one-time effort but an ongoing process. The market will continue to evolve, and staying ahead means regularly updating your understanding of your audience and the competitive landscape.

By integrating these insights into their business and marketing strategies, Mr & Mrs Egypt is well-positioned to not only meet but exceed the expectations of a discerning, high-end clientele, securing a strong foothold in the luxury travel market to Egypt.

 For a deeper dive into the data and methods discussed, full reports and resources are available in the download section of this book.

Creating the strategy

With a wealth of data and insights at our fingertips, we now move on to the most exciting phase of the project—building a strategy that we believe will drive bookings for Mr & Mrs Egypt.

The following section outlines a wide range of ideas we proposed to Carol and Atef. Not every suggestion was implemented, but I think it's important to showcase the full breadth of our thinking. Of course, there were a few challenges to navigate along the way. For instance, Carol, and I know she won't mind me saying this, was initially hesitant to appear in videos—a key component of the strategy we envisioned.

Before diving into the full strategy, let's take a moment to explore some of these challenges...

The challenges

The credibility gap

One of the biggest challenges Mr & Mrs Egypt faces as a new brand is establishing trust within a highly competitive sector. Trust is a key factor for customers when booking high-ticket experiences, particularly in the tourism industry where travellers are often making significant financial and emotional investments. With no existing online reviews and a fresh brand identity, building credibility will be a crucial focus in the early stages.

The upside, however, is that while Mr & Mrs Egypt is a new brand,

Carol and Atef have been successfully operating their previous brand for over 30 years. This extensive experience in the industry provides a strong foundation for building trust. Leveraging their decades of expertise and well-established relationships will be key in reassuring potential customers that, while the brand may be new, the team behind it is not.

The content on the site must reflect this expertise, and we must create a strategy that will fast-track this process. We'll need to create high-quality content at a rapid pace to ensure the site competes effectively in the market.

Customer needs

Crafting a strategy that caters to various customer needs is essential. Different users will interact with the website in different ways. Some visitors prefer to immerse themselves in detailed research, comparing every option before making a decision. Others, however, may want a more streamlined experience, quickly finding what they need to enquire or book. Additionally, some customers seek a guided experience, relying on the website to walk them through every step, while others come in with a clear idea and simply need the tools to bring their vision to life.

Balancing these diverse user preferences is key to ensuring that Mr & Mrs Egypt can meet every potential customer where they are. The website must accommodate both types of visitors seamlessly, offering comprehensive information without overwhelming those who want a simpler approach.

Lack of good visuals

Visuals will also play a huge role here and unfortunately, Carol and Atef don't have much in this regard.

Customers are unlikely to book high-ticket experiences without compelling images and videos that evoke the beauty and allure of Egypt. For Mr & Mrs Egypt to succeed, building an extensive collection of original visuals will be critical. These should showcase everything from iconic landmarks like the Pyramids and the Nile River to the more intimate moments of cultural experiences showing people.

By offering a visual journey that captures the essence of their tours, Mr & Mrs Egypt can build trust with potential customers, making them feel confident in spending thousands of dollars on a once-in-a-lifetime trip.

Finding the right language and messaging

Finding the right language to describe the level of service and customisation they offer is also key. From earlier research, we know that American audiences don't respond well to the term "bespoke," even though it's popular in the UK. Similarly, while "luxury" is synonymous with high-end travel, it doesn't attract significant search volume.

Instead, terms like "private" and "boutique" have gained traction and may resonate more with the target audience. Refining this messaging will be a process of trial and error, but it's important to adjust the language early on to align with customer expectations and search behaviour.

Avoiding overload

Another significant challenge they face is communicating the extensive customisation options available to their customers. Custom travel experiences are inherently complex, and showcasing all the possibilities without overwhelming the user requires a delicate balance. The key is to make the flexibility and personalisation of the tours clear while guiding customers through an intuitive user journey.

The goal here will be to simplify the decision-making process for users, whether they are looking for pre-packaged tours or seeking to build a completely custom experience.

Getting creative: brainstorming marketing ideas

Now, we're going to dive into a session of idea generation for Mr & Mrs Egypt.

"Brainstorm" might not be the perfect term—it's more of a creative "braindump." Why? Because at this stage, we're not yet diving deep into the customer journey; instead, we're throwing ideas on the table—whether it's about content, strategy, promotions, videos, or anything else that comes to mind. Not every idea will make it to the final cut, and that's okay. The point here is that no idea is off-limits. It's better to filter and refine further down the line rather than dismiss potential opportunities too early.

I'd recommend grabbing a stack of Post-it notes and letting your creativity run wild. There's something about physically writing down ideas that helps get the creative juices flowing, more so than staring at a screen. Think about all the ways you can promote your business, how to communicate with your customers, and what types of content might resonate. Consider who in your business is best suited to deliver that content.

For now, keep it high-level—just get those initial ideas down on Post-its and stick them on the wall. From there, you'll be able to see the bigger picture and start shaping your strategy.

Below are a few ideas we came up with for Mr & Mrs Egypt.

Key areas we've identified

We know Mr & Mrs Egypt needs to build a strong online presence from scratch, so a website overhaul has to be the first big action point. We need to make sure the user experience is seamless—particularly when it comes to booking. But what will really set this website apart?

During this process we knew incorporating video content should be front and centre—things like a "Safe Egypt" series, or "A Woman's Guide to Egypt." These videos would not only put potential female customers at ease but also establish trust right from the start. That's one for the top of our to-do list.

We've talked about creating regular blog posts as a way to drive organic traffic and build credibility. But we need to make it more than just surface-level content. Ideas like destination guides or posts addressing female travel in Egypt could work well to capture niche search terms. Maybe we could also produce content around lesser-known gems in Egypt—this could appeal to more adventurous travellers or those looking for something beyond the typical tourist experience.

On the social media side, we've mentioned Instagram and Facebook, but Pinterest has also come up as a potential platform for visually driven storytelling. A good fit, especially when it comes to showcasing stunning Egyptian landscapes and custom itineraries. Pinterest boards, full of rich visuals, could link directly back to the blog or landing pages on the site—perfect for driving traffic.

Another idea we floated was launching a travel guide podcast. Audio content could be a great way to engage potential travellers on a more personal level, and each episode could focus on topics like hidden gems in Egypt, expert travel tips, or interviews with locals. Plus, podcasts are great for repurposing content—you could take snippets of each episode and turn them into blog posts or social media clips. So, that's something worth exploring.

Experimenting with paid advertising and lead generation

We also started thinking about how to bring in potential leads. Of course, organic traffic is crucial, but we can't ignore paid advertising—we're talking Facebook and Instagram ads targeting female travellers, luxury tourists, and those interested in safety-conscious travel experiences. We've also brainstormed ideas for a lead magnet—something like a downloadable "Top Books on Egypt" guide could be an easy way to collect email addresses and start nurturing leads.

And what about competitions? One idea we tossed around was running a Facebook competition—offering a custom Egypt tour as the prize. This could not only help generate buzz around the brand but also boost social engagement and build the email list. It's something we'd want to trial at the right time when we've built up a bit more brand awareness.

Building trust and authority

With Mr & Mrs Egypt being a new brand, they're starting from scratch in terms of reviews and online reputation. However, with their 30 years of experience behind the scenes, we can leverage that history. The website should tell this story—emphasising their decades of expertise in Egyptian travel and positioning them as trusted authorities. Testimonials from past clients could be brought over from their previous business to establish credibility right away.

But what other trust-building tactics can we brainstorm? We've talked about pushing video testimonials and potentially offering early customers an incentive to leave detailed reviews online. Those initial reviews are going to be essential for establishing social proof early on.

Seo and targeted messaging

Finally, we threw out some ideas around SEO and the need to get the right terms in place from the beginning. There's been some debate around the use of words like "bespoke," which doesn't seem to resonate as well with the American audience. Instead, we're thinking of leaning into terms like "private" or "boutique," which are trending more in recent years. This messaging will need to be refined over time, but it's something we'll continue to tweak as we roll out the strategy.

We also touched on targeting niche keywords like "female solo travel in Egypt" and "luxury Nile cruises" to ensure we're capturing the right audience. This will be part of a larger content optimisation strategy that we'll implement across blog posts, landing pages, and videos.

Guerilla marketing ideas

When it comes to guerrilla marketing for Mr & Mrs Egypt, we need to think outside the box and create something truly memorable. Given that their customers would book months in advance and from the comfort of their own homes, our approach should focus on making an impact in key cities and at touchpoints where potential customers are thinking about their next big adventure. The goal is to plant the seed of interest in Egypt in a way that's impossible to ignore.

One idea is to create Egyptian-inspired pop-up installations in high-traffic areas of target cities. Imagine stumbling upon a life-size pyramid replica or an immersive desert tent experience while rushing through a train station or shopping mall. These pop-ups could be designed to encourage interaction—perhaps there's a designated photo-op area where passersby can take pictures against the backdrop of the pyramids, sharing them on social media with a branded hashtag for a chance to win a tour of Egypt.

Taking this idea further, we could develop a mysterious, Egypt-themed treasure hunt across the same cities. Participants follow a series of ancient Egyptian clues, leading them to hidden landmarks or local businesses. The treasure hunt ends with an exciting prize—perhaps a travel gift voucher or a free custom tour with Mr & Mrs Egypt. This strategy not only draws attention to the brand but creates an immersive experience that sparks a sense of adventure.

An Egyptian-themed flash mob taking over a busy public space. Dancers dressed as pharaohs, gods, or ancient explorers could perform a captivating routine, catching people by surprise. The performance could culminate in the dancers handing out branded postcards that include a QR code linked to a discount on tours, or perhaps even an exclusive travel guide to Egypt. The energy and spectacle of the flash mob would not only attract attention but also offer a tangible way for people to learn more about Mr & Mrs Egypt and consider booking a tour.

I did say no idea was off the table remember!

Next steps

So, where does this leave us? We came up with so many ideas that it would fill a book on its own, so you can see the majority of our ideas in the download section, including over 100 blog titles and topics! This was before the advent of AI tools like ChatGPT which now makes this process so much easier.

Grab your team, or if you do not have a team, gather friends and family round for a few beers or glasses of wine and make a night of it. Remember, there is no stupid idea so let those creative juices flow.

Crafting a 12-month strategy

With the brainstorming stage behind us, it's time to take the ideas we believe will make the most impact and develop a comprehensive marketing strategy for Mr & Mrs Egypt. This plan will be a roadmap to grow the brand, drive engagement, and convert leads into bookings.

To make the strategy manageable and focused, we'll divide it into quarterly phases, with each stage of the process targeting the first three parts of the customer journey—Dreaming, Planning, and Booking. The rest of the journey will be addressed later.

I would also recommend that the strategy you create follows the first three parts of the consumer journey; Dreaming, Planning and Booking. We will look at the rest of the journey later.

Here's how we can bring this strategy to life over the next 12 months.

Quarter one: laying the foundation

In the first quarter, we're setting the groundwork. This is about ensuring the digital presence is solid, visually engaging, and capable of building trust with prospective customers.

The goal here is to establish the digital foundation, build awareness, and initiate engagement.

Website overhaul

The website is the core of the entire strategy. A complete overhaul of the site is essential to ensure that it's user-friendly, mobile-responsive, and optimised for both search engines and bookings. The user experience (UX) needs to be streamlined, particularly for those ready to book, with minimal friction. We'll integrate key video content to immediately engage visitors and help them feel confident in their decision to travel to Egypt with Mr & Mrs Egypt.

Dreaming stage

In the first quarter, our goal is to capture the imagination of potential customers while they are in the Dreaming phase. At this stage, travellers are exploring destination ideas, inspired by the allure of adventure and new experiences. To effectively engage with these potential visitors, Mr & Mrs Egypt must create content that evokes strong emotions and showcases the beauty and uniqueness of Egypt as a dream-worthy destination.

Written content hubs

A key strategy is to develop SEO-rich content hubs that cater to those in the dreaming phase. We'll create a "Dreaming of Egypt" section on the website, featuring guides and inspiration articles about Egypt's hidden gems, cultural experiences, and compelling reasons why Egypt should be at the top of their travel list. This section will serve as an aspirational resource for travellers and be optimised for search terms such as "must-see places in Egypt," "reasons to visit Egypt," and "luxury travel destinations."

By focusing on these terms, we will position Mr & Mrs Egypt as a trusted source for inspiration, helping potential travellers picture themselves exploring this exotic location.

Video content hubs

We'll also build a hub of video content designed to capture the visual imagination of travellers. Video is especially powerful during the Dreaming stage, as it brings the destination to life in a way that words alone can't.

Key series like Safe Egypt and A Woman's Guide to Egypt will be featured prominently, with videos optimised for YouTube and Google search. Each video will be carefully titled, tagged, and described using keywords like "safe travel to Egypt for women" or "female solo travel in Egypt." By doing this, we'll ensure that these videos appear when potential customers are searching for Egypt-related content.

In addition, we can repurpose the written content ideas from the "Dreaming of Egypt" section into engaging video formats, allowing us to reach different audiences who prefer visual storytelling.

Social media campaigns

To further engage customers in the Dreaming stage, we'll share snippets from the video series and other inspirational content across Facebook, Instagram, and Pinterest. Social platforms are ideal for capturing attention through striking imagery and emotional messaging. Our focus will be on portraying Egypt as a magical and safe destination, highlighting its beauty, culture, and unique travel experiences. By showing Egypt through this lens, we'll inspire travellers to begin seriously considering it for their next adventure.

In addition to the organic and paid content, a powerful way to enhance social media efforts is by collaborating with influencers. Partnering with a travel influencer who has a strong, engaged following could amplify Mr & Mrs Egypt's reach. This influencer could be someone who specialises in luxury travel or cultural exploration and is aligned with the brand's values.

By sharing their own experiences of Egypt, perhaps through an exclusive trip curated by Mr & Mrs Egypt, the influencer can act as a trusted voice, showing their audience the appeal of travelling to Egypt in a personal and engaging way. This influencer collaboration will bring authenticity to the campaign, creating an emotional connection with potential customers and driving them into the dreaming phase of their travel journey.

Paid ads to expand reach

To complement our organic efforts and further extend Mr & Mrs Egypt's reach, we will introduce targeted awareness campaigns on Facebook and Instagram, aimed at affluent travellers in the US and UK who are in the early stages of planning their trips. These paid ads will form a critical part of our overall strategy, aligning with the first three stages of the consumer journey: Dreaming, Planning, and Booking.

The primary focus of these ads will be on custom tours, which offer a unique and personal way to explore Egypt. By honing in on this offering, we can speak directly to travellers seeking tailored, high-end experiences.

For the Dreaming stage, our aim is to capture attention and drive users toward top-of-the-funnel content. These will be educational and inspirational pieces designed to pique curiosity and stir excitement about Egypt. Content such as "How to Choose the Best Nile Cruise in Egypt," "A Guide to the Best Restaurants in Egypt," and "6 Awesome Places in Cairo That Most Visitors Don't See" will help potential customers start envisioning their trip.

In addition, we'll release a video ad titled Beyond the Pyramids, emphasising that Egypt has much more to offer than just its famous pyramids, encouraging travellers to see the lesser-known wonders of the country.

Planning stage

As we capture interest, we'll guide potential customers toward the Planning phase. In this stage, they'll be looking for more detailed information about Egypt and how to turn their dream trip into reality. This is where content, videos, blog posts, and targeted paid ads will help guide them through the research and decision-making process.

Written content & videos

The planning stage requires content that addresses logistical concerns and inspires confidence. Potential travellers are thinking about the details: where to go, where to stay, and how to customise their experience.

"How to Plan Your Custom Trip to Egypt": A step-by-step guide that walks potential customers through the process of customising their trip. Each video could cover different aspects, such as selecting destinations within Egypt, choosing accommodation, and creating bespoke itineraries that suit their needs.

"Best Times to Visit Egypt": This will help planners understand when to visit based on weather, local festivals, and peak travel seasons. By addressing their concerns and providing clear advice, this content will help customers move from research to decision-making.

"Frequently Asked Questions About Egypt Travel": A Q&A-style content piece answering common concerns around visas, transportation, cultural etiquette, and safety. This will serve as an invaluable resource for those in the planning phase, offering practical information that reassures them as they consider booking.

"Private and Luxury Travel in Egypt": This will highlight the premium services Mr & Mrs Egypt offers, focusing on luxury tours, Nile cruises, and private experiences. For travellers considering high-end travel, this video will present Egypt as a destination that caters to their preferences.

High-intent paid ad campaigns

The planning phase is the perfect time to begin running retargeting ads to those who interacted with the ads and content from the dreaming stage ads. These ads will help potential customers find the information they need. These ads should also focus on high-intent travellers who are actively researching their trip.

As travellers progress to the Planning stage, the focus will shift to video content that introduces the faces behind the brand—Carol and Atef. A 'Meet Carol and Atef' video will showcase their expertise and passion, directing viewers to a dedicated landing page with two clear calls to action: a contact form and a bookable calendar for scheduling a consultation. This personal touch builds trust and connection, key elements for converting high-value travellers.

Additionally, we'll launch two videos that address common concerns directly, especially around safety. These 'Is Egypt Safe?' ads are specifically designed to appeal to the female travel market, offering reassurance and positioning Mr & Mrs Egypt as a trusted partner in planning safe, luxurious travel experiences.

Google Search Ads will also be launched, targeting specific high-intent keywords such as "luxury Egypt tours," "custom Egypt travel," and "Egypt travel planning." These ads will drive traffic to key landing pages where users can explore itineraries, accommodation options, and custom tours.

Pinterest Ads will also be considered since many planners use Pinterest for travel inspiration, we'll look to run Pinterest ads showcasing custom itineraries and beautiful, visual itineraries to further engage those in the planning phase.

Blog posts

Blog content during the planning phase will focus on helping customers understand the full experience, offering inspiration while providing practical tips for building their perfect trip. These posts will be rich in SEO-optimised keywords to capture search traffic.

"Luxury Egypt Tours: A Complete Guide to Custom Travel" – This post will provide an in-depth look at how Mr & Mrs Egypt offers bespoke tours, outlining the advantages of a custom itinerary.

"How to Travel Safely in Egypt: Tips for Female Travellers" – This article will provide reassurance to those concerned about safety, offering practical advice for solo female travellers. By addressing these concerns, Mr & Mrs Egypt can position itself as a trusted resource.

"Exploring Egypt's Hidden Gems: Off-the-Beaten-Path Adventures" – Highlight some of Egypt's lesser-known but equally stunning locations, like Siwa Oasis or the White Desert, giving potential customers a reason to explore beyond the usual tourist destinations.

"A Packing Guide for Your Egyptian Adventure" – A practical blog post offering packing tips for various activities (from desert treks to city tours) and seasons, helping customers feel well-prepared and excited for their journey.

SEO

SEO optimisation is crucial at this stage to ensure that the website and its content rank highly when potential travellers search for Egypt-related travel information.

Focus on optimising for high-intent keywords like "luxury Egypt tours," "custom Egypt travel," and "safe travel Egypt." These terms will align with what planners are searching for as they get closer to booking.

Internal linking: Create a network of internal links between planning-focused blog posts and videos, making it easier for users to find the information they need and helping search engines crawl the site more efficiently.

Featured snippets: Structure blog posts and FAQs to target featured snippets on Google, ensuring Mr & Mrs Egypt's content is prominently displayed for key searches such as "how to plan a custom tour in Egypt" or "best time to visit Egypt."

Lead magnets

In the Planning stage, potential customers are looking for useful, actionable resources to help them prepare for their trip to Egypt. This is where lead magnets come into play—valuable, downloadable content that not only helps travellers but also captures their contact information, allowing Mr & Mrs Egypt to nurture these leads through email marketing and other channels.

One of the key lead magnets could be a Travel Checklist for Egypt. This downloadable PDF would cover everything a traveller needs to plan their trip, from packing essentials and visa requirements to tips on cultural etiquette and health precautions. By offering this checklist in exchange for an email address, we can collect high-quality leads while providing immediate value to potential customers. The checklist can also be tailored for different types of travellers, such as solo travellers, families, or luxury tourists, making it more relevant and appealing.

A second lead magnet idea is a 'Top 10 Hidden Gems of Egypt guide'. This beautifully designed document would introduce potential customers to lesser-known but stunning locations in Egypt, reinforcing the brand's expertise in crafting unique and unforgettable trips. The guide would also feature high-quality imagery and travel tips to spark excitement about exploring off-the-beaten-path destinations.

By creating and promoting these lead magnets through the website and paid ads, we can attract highly engaged potential customers who are already in the planning phase, gathering valuable leads for future follow-up.

Booking stage

After guiding potential customers through the Dreaming and Planning stages, our next focus is to ensure we're fully prepared for the Booking stage. This phase is where we convert interest into action, encouraging travellers to make enquiries and start the booking process.

Call-to-action elements

To facilitate bookings, we need to integrate strong, clear calls-to-action (CTAs) throughout the website. The goal is to make it as simple as possible for customers to reach out and take the next step, whether that's making an enquiry, booking a call, or filling out a form.

Bookable Calendars: Offering tools like Google Calendar or Calendly will allow potential customers to easily schedule a call with Carol. This personalised approach gives customers the opportunity to have their questions answered directly, building trust while streamlining the booking process. Customers can pick a time that suits them, adding a level of convenience that enhances their experience and increases the likelihood of conversion.

Email Form Options: For those who may not be ready to hop on a call, we'll also include easy-to-use email enquiry forms on key landing pages. These forms will be simple yet effective, asking for important details like travel dates, areas of interest, and any specific questions they have. The form provides a lower-commitment option, allowing more hesitant users to engage at their own pace.

By providing both a straightforward way to book a consultation and a lower-pressure email form, we cater to different types of customers, making it easy for them to move forward with an enquiry in a way that suits their style.

Paid ads

As we transition into the Booking phase, the strategy shifts to a more direct approach, focusing on clear calls to action that target users who have already engaged with the website or interacted with Planning stage content. The goal at this point is to encourage potential customers to take that final step—making a booking.

These ads will serve as timely reminders, promoting special offers or exclusive tours to create a sense of urgency and push customers toward conversion.

A central piece of this strategy will be a video featuring Carol herself, inviting users to 'Book a consultation with us'. This personal touch is designed to build on the trust established in earlier stages and drive potential travellers to the custom tour page, where they can explore a range of tailored itineraries. By leading users directly to a page focused on bespoke experiences, we can further highlight the personalised service Mr & Mrs Egypt offers, making it easier for them to commit to a booking.

To add variety and appeal to different segments of our audience, two additional ads will be introduced during this stage. The first, 'Write Your Own Adventure', will continue to focus on the custom tour offering, emphasising the flexibility and uniqueness of crafting a personalised Egyptian journey. The second, 'Book an 18-Day Egypt Luxury Experience', will highlight a more structured option, showcasing an all-inclusive luxury tour designed to appeal to travellers looking for a comprehensive, high-end experience.

This mix of ads will cater to different preferences, ensuring that both custom and pre-designed tour options are promoted effectively.

In addition to video ads, we will launch Google Display Ads to retarget users who showed interest during the Planning phase. These ads will guide them back to key landing pages that focus on booking custom Egypt tours. They will feature compelling offers, unique itineraries, and testimonials from satisfied customers, all designed to reassure potential clients that Mr & Mrs Egypt is the right choice for their luxury travel experience. These reminders, paired with clear calls to action, will help convert those still on the fence into committed bookers.

By employing a targeted, multi-faceted approach in the Booking stage, we can effectively nudge potential customers toward making a decision, whether they're drawn to the personalised allure of custom tours or the convenience and luxury of a pre-designed itinerary. This stage is all about closing the deal, and the combination of direct messaging, video storytelling, and strategic retargeting ads is designed to do just that.

Email marketing

To keep potential customers engaged and inspired as they inch closer to booking, we'll launch a more frequent email marketing approach. A weekly email newsletter will keep Mr & Mrs Egypt top of mind and provide ongoing inspiration during the planning process.

Weekly Newsletter: We'll send a weekly newsletter that focuses on keeping potential customers inspired and engaged. Each week's email will feature new highlights from the video series, blog posts, and planning guides, ensuring recipients receive fresh and engaging content. These emails will provide planning tips, special offers, and travel inspiration to nudge customers toward finalising their booking. Each email will include clear CTAs, such as "Schedule a Call" or "Start Planning Your Custom Tour," making it easy for recipients to take action.

Abandoned Enquiry Follow-ups: For customers who started an enquiry but didn't finish the process, we'll create an automated follow-up email sequence to bring them back into the booking flow. These follow-ups will offer additional details, testimonials, or limited-time offers to help overcome any hesitation and encourage completing the booking.

Tracking and monitoring

As we establish the foundation of Mr & Mrs Egypt's digital presence, it's crucial to measure key metrics to gauge early engagement and brand awareness. At this stage, we'll focus on tracking website traffic, particularly increases in visits to key landing pages created for the Dreaming and Planning stages. Google Analytics will be essential for monitoring overall traffic, session durations, and bounce rates.

For social media, engagement rates such as likes, shares, and comments will indicate how well our content is resonating with users in the Dreaming phase. It's important to track the performance of video snippets and blog shares across Facebook, Instagram, and Pinterest, ensuring we're reaching our target audience effectively.

Additionally, we'll begin monitoring email sign-ups from any lead magnets or newsletters, ensuring the planning stage content is generating interest. Tracking these early signs of engagement will help us refine our content strategy in real time.

Quarter two: growth and engagement

In the second quarter, our focus shifts to building momentum. This phase is all about increasing engagement with potential customers and capturing leads, laying the groundwork for converting interest into bookings. By deepening connections with those in the Dreaming, Planning, and Booking stages, we'll build on the foundational work from Quarter One.

Dreaming stage

As we continue to capture the imaginations of potential customers in the Dreaming stage, we'll amplify our efforts by integrating engaging visual content and leveraging user-generated stories. This phase is all about sustaining excitement and keeping Egypt top of mind as travellers dream of their next adventure.

Social media campaigns

This quarter, we'll focus heavily on social proof and user-generated content. Encouraging past customers to share their experiences, photos, and stories from their trips to Egypt will not only engage potential travellers but also build trust. Showcasing authentic experiences from real people helps to spark the imagination of future travellers. We'll also continue promoting visually stunning content across Facebook, Instagram, and Pinterest, particularly short video clips from the Safe Egypt series and A Woman's Guide to Egypt.

Videos and paid ads

While the previous ad campaigns will continue to run, to broaden our reach, we'll expand the distribution of the Guide to Egypt's Lesser-Known Spots video series. By using YouTube Ads, we can target new audiences who are still in the early stages of exploring travel ideas. These ads will serve as an entry point to more detailed content on the Mr & Mrs Egypt website, helping to move customers from dreaming about Egypt to actively considering it for their next trip.

User-generated content and hashtag campaigns

Nothing resonates more with potential travellers than seeing real experiences from fellow travellers. By showcasing authentic stories, photos, and videos from past customers, we can create a sense of community and credibility around the brand.

To tap into this, we'll look to introduce a hashtag campaign across social media platforms like Instagram, Facebook, and Pinterest. The goal is to encourage past customers to share their experiences of Egypt using a dedicated hashtag, such as #MyEgyptAdventure or #ExploreWithMrAndMrsEgypt. This not only provides an opportunity for users to relive their travels but also allows Mr & Mrs Egypt to curate a wealth of organic content that can be reshared on the company's social channels.

As part of the campaign, we could run a contest or offer a small incentive, like a discount on future tours, for the best photo or story shared using the hashtag. This kind of engagement encourages interaction and helps create a steady flow of new content that showcases Egypt through the eyes of real travellers, making the destination even more relatable and desirable to prospective customers still in the Dreaming stage.

Planning stage

As travellers move from dreaming to actively planning their trip, our goal is to provide even more detailed and useful content that helps them build a custom itinerary. The second quarter will emphasise creating resources that answer practical questions while keeping the sense of excitement alive.

Content creation

We'll continue publishing high-value blog posts that offer inspiration and detailed planning tips. For example, content that highlights cultural landmarks, hidden gems, and practical travel advice will help planners envision the finer details of their trip.

Topics like Top Books Based on Egypt will provide in-depth insights for those wanting to deepen their understanding of the destination. Each post will be optimised for SEO, ensuring it ranks well for planning-related search terms like "planning a trip to Egypt" or "custom Egypt itineraries."

Lunch podcast

Podcasts will be an important tool to immerse potential customers in the culture and experiences of Egypt. We'll release episodes that focus on topics like female travel in Egypt and cultural highlights such as local festivals or significant historical sites. These episodes will not only inform but also help listeners imagine themselves walking through Egypt's markets or exploring its ancient ruins.

Promoted organically through social media and paid Google Ads, these podcasts will drive engagement with our brand.

Pinterest campaigns

We'll use Pinterest's visually-driven nature to promote beautiful, shareable pins that inspire users to plan their Egyptian adventure. These pins will link back to relevant blog posts, driving traffic to our site and keeping users in the planning phase engaged.

Booking stage

By Quarter Two, we aim to transition more of our audience from planning into early bookings. This stage is crucial for converting interest into action, and we'll achieve that by providing clear, reassuring content and delivering attractive offers.

Lead generation ads

Using dynamic retargeting ads on Facebook, we'll continue to target users who have visited the Mr & Mrs Egypt website or engaged with the content but haven't yet made a booking. These ads will serve as a reminder, showcasing attractive offers, luxury packages, or exclusive itineraries to encourage them to take that next step toward booking their trip.

Email marketing

This quarter, we'll launch a lead nurturing campaign aimed at the new leads we've gathered through our paid ads. These email sequences will guide potential customers through the final stages of their decision-making process.

Weekly emails will continue to offer exclusive deals, personalised itineraries, and testimonials from past travellers, providing the reassurance and incentives needed to push them toward booking. By keeping these communications regular and focused on providing value, we'll ensure potential customers remain engaged until they are ready to commit.

By refining the user journey in Quarter Two, we'll build upon the momentum from Quarter One, moving customers deeper into the Planning and Booking phases. Our strategy will be to continuously inspire, provide clear and helpful resources, and gently nudge potential customers towards converting their dream of visiting Egypt into a reality.

Tracking and monitoring

As we move into Quarter Two and ramp up our content and lead-generation campaigns, we'll shift focus to measuring interaction with content and lead-generation efforts. Metrics like click-through rates (CTR) on social media and engagement rates for podcasts and blog posts will show us how well we're guiding users from dreaming to planning.

We'll also track the performance of our lead generation ads, focusing on the number of email sign-ups we're gaining from the downloadable guides or competition entries. Our email nurturing campaigns will need close attention as well, where open rates and click rates will tell us if we're delivering value to subscribers.

By assessing these metrics, we'll be able to determine if the audience is moving through the customer journey as expected and make adjustments as needed to our messaging or targeting.

Quarter three: lead generation and conversions

As we move into Quarter Three, our focus sharpens on generating leads and driving conversions. The groundwork laid in the earlier phases will now serve as a launchpad for turning interest into action, pushing customers toward booking their dream trip to Egypt. At this point, our strategy should build on engagement with targeted, high-intent efforts, using a combination of new content, competitions, and personalised offers.

Dreaming stage

By the third quarter, those still in the Dreaming phase should have strong brand awareness of Mr & Mrs Egypt. Our goal will be to continue nurturing that connection with visually compelling and emotionally driven content, keeping Egypt front of mind as a top destination.

Competition campaign

To capture fresh attention and generate excitement, we'll launch a Facebook competition to win a custom Egypt tour. Competitions are a powerful tool for engaging new audiences and providing a fun, interactive way to bring people into our marketing ecosystem.

This campaign will appeal to those still dreaming about their next adventure and help build a sense of connection with the Mr & Mrs Egypt brand. As a bonus, this competition will also capture a wave of new leads who may not have been considering Egypt but are now intrigued by the opportunity.

Social media & video content

We'll continue to push visually rich content on social media, sharing user-generated stories and leveraging the success of our Safe Egypt and A Woman's Guide to Egypt video series. By consistently showing Egypt's beauty and cultural depth, we'll keep engaging customers emotionally, feeding their sense of adventure and wanderlust.

Planning stage

In the third quarter, we'll double down on building trust with customers in the Planning phase. They're already seriously considering Egypt, so we'll provide them with the kind of content that reinforces their decision and makes them feel confident about choosing both Egypt and Mr & Mrs Egypt for their journey.

Blogs posts

Content at this stage needs to be conversion-driven, giving potential travellers all the information they need to finalise their plans. Blog posts will focus on key topics like customer testimonials, detailed Nile cruise guides, and planning tips for luxury Egypt tours. For example, we'll write about "What to Expect from a Luxury Nile Cruise" or "How to Plan the Ultimate Custom Tour in Egypt," providing the reassurance and inspiration necessary for converting those on the fence.

Podcast strategy

Our podcast episodes will delve deeper into Egypt's most sought-after experiences, such as luxury Nile cruises, private desert tours, and exclusive cultural encounters. We'll promote these episodes through organic social media and Google Ads, positioning them as valuable resources for those in the midst of planning their trip.

Google search ads

At this point, we'll ramp up the targeting of high-intent keywords like "custom Egypt tours," "luxury Nile cruises," and "private Egypt itineraries." These search ads will capture customers actively planning their trip and ready to move from researching to booking. The ads will direct them to detailed landing pages that showcase why Mr & Mrs Egypt is the best choice for their bespoke journey. Booking Stage

The primary focus will be converting those leads we've nurtured into actual bookings. This is the phase where our efforts will shift from engagement to decisive action, ensuring customers feel confident enough to commit to their Egypt adventure.

Lead generation follow-up

After the competition campaign from the Dreaming phase, we'll follow up with all participants via email. These emails will offer exclusive booking discounts or value-added perks (such as complimentary tour upgrades) for those who are ready to take the next step. The goal is to turn the excitement from the competition into tangible bookings, leveraging the interest generated.

Retargeting ads

We'll make strong use of Facebook and Instagram retargeting ads to convert individuals who have visited the website or engaged with our content but have yet to make a booking. These ads will showcase newly available tours, limited-time offers, and discounted packages designed to push them towards conversion. By targeting this engaged audience, we'll keep Egypt top of mind and use urgency (e.g., limited spots or early bird pricing) to drive them to act.

Email campaigns

To convert past customers into repeat bookings, we'll run a loyalty campaign offering discounts or special experiences to those who have previously travelled with Mr & Mrs Egypt. This campaign will position Egypt as an ever-evolving destination with new experiences, making the case that a return trip offers something fresh and exciting. Personalised email content will include exclusive offers and VIP packages, making past customers feel valued and incentivising them to rebook.

By the end of Quarter Three, our focus on lead generation, retargeting, and personalised follow-ups should result in a marked increase in conversions, as well as a growing pool of loyal, repeat customers. Through this multi-layered approach, we'll turn potential travellers into booked customers, capitalising on the momentum from the previous quarters.

Tracking and monitoring

Quarter Three is all about generating leads and pushing conversions. During this period, our primary metrics will shift towards conversion rates—how many of the leads we've generated are converting into bookings or strong inquiries.

We'll track lead-to-conversion ratios from our paid ads and retargeting campaigns, ensuring that our efforts in the Booking stage are paying off. For email marketing, conversion tracking will show how effective our re-engagement and loyalty campaigns are at turning past customers or interested leads into actual bookings.

At this stage, metrics such as abandoned enquiry follow-ups and retargeting performance will be key indicators of success. If we notice any gaps in the customer journey, we'll adjust our messaging or offer additional incentives to close more sales.

Quarter four: conversions and refinement

As we move into the final quarter of the year, the focus sharpens on maximising bookings for 2025 and refining our content strategy to ensure it continues to perform at its best. By this stage, we will have built a strong foundation and engaged audiences across various stages of the customer journey. Now, the emphasis shifts to converting leads into bookings and fine-tuning our efforts based on the data and insights we've gathered throughout the year.

Dreaming stage

Even as the year draws to a close, we must continue to inspire and capture the imagination of travellers still in the Dreaming phase. Emotional storytelling and stunning visuals will remain key, keeping Mr & Mrs Egypt top of mind as travellers begin to think about their adventures for the year ahead.

Holiday campaigns

A major opportunity for the Dreaming stage in Quarter Four will be running holiday-themed campaigns. We'll position Egypt tours as the perfect holiday gift or a special getaway for early 2025. Social media platforms like Facebook, Instagram, and Pinterest will be our main advertising channels, where we'll use compelling imagery and messaging like "Gift an Egypt Adventure" to spark interest in purchasing a trip for a loved one or themselves.

Additionally, this campaign will highlight Egypt's unique experiences that could be enjoyed in early 2025, encouraging customers to start thinking about their travel plans for the coming year. By maintaining momentum in the Dreaming phase through these emotionally engaging ads, we'll set the stage for strong early conversions in 2025.

Planning stage

By Quarter Four, we'll have amassed a substantial amount of content for the Planning phase, but the focus now will be on refining that content to encourage bookings for the 2025 travel season. We'll continue to guide customers through the planning process with informative and reassuring content, tailored to address any lingering questions or concerns they may have.

Content creation

To push potential customers further along the booking journey, we'll focus on creating highly conversion-driven blog posts. Pieces like "Why Book with Mr & Mrs Egypt for 2025?" and "Customer Stories: A Trip to Egypt" will help build confidence in choosing Mr & Mrs Egypt. Customer stories, in particular, will be a powerful tool for demonstrating real experiences, showing potential travellers the unique and customised experiences they can expect.

By using real testimonials and detailed itineraries, we'll position Egypt as not just a dream destination, but one that's within reach.

SEO refinement

At this stage, it's critical to revisit top-performing blog posts and landing pages to further optimise them for search engines. We'll assess which keywords and pieces of content have driven the most traffic and conversions throughout the year, refining the SEO strategy to push these pages higher in search rankings. By adjusting meta titles, descriptions, and internal linking structures, we'll ensure Mr & Mrs Egypt is capturing high-intent search traffic from planners actively researching their 2025 travel plans. This process will be crucial for driving organic traffic and keeping potential customers engaged as they plan their trips.

Booking stage

The final quarter of the year will be all about converting those leads who are on the verge of booking. We'll use a combination of retargeting campaigns and personalised email marketing to encourage customers to take the final step and secure their booking for 2025. The messaging here will be urgent, focusing on early-bird deals and exclusive offers to create a sense of urgency.

Paid ads

We'll significantly ramp up Facebook and Instagram retargeting campaigns, targeting users who have engaged with our content, visited the site, or joined our email list but haven't yet booked. These retargeting ads will feature exclusive early-bird deals for 2025, along with testimonials from past travellers to instil confidence and drive bookings. Offering time-sensitive promotions, such as limited spots or exclusive discounts, will encourage customers to commit before the year ends.

Email marketing

A weekly email campaign will focus on last-minute promotions, targeting leads who are close to booking but haven't yet taken the leap. These emails will highlight early-bird offers, feature content from the Safe Egypt video series, and share customer stories to inspire confidence. This targeted approach will help push those who are on the fence towards finalising their booking, ensuring a strong start to the 2025 season.

Abandoned enquiry follow-ups

For potential customers who have made an enquiry but not completed the booking process, we'll run an automated follow-up email series. These emails will gently nudge the customer to take action, offering additional incentives like extra value-added perks (e.g., a complimentary guided tour or a free cultural experience) to close the booking.

Adding urgency

As we push to convert leads into 2025 bookings, creating a sense of urgency will be key. One powerful way to do this is by adding a 'hurry' to key landing pages that feature early-bird deals or exclusive offers. Whether it's for a limited-time discount on a custom Egypt tour or an exclusive upgrade offer, adding a hurry creates a psychological push, motivating users to act quickly.

By focusing on conversions and refinement, Quarter Four will ensure that Mr & Mrs Egypt finishes the year strong, with a full pipeline of 2025 bookings and a highly optimised content and marketing strategy. Through targeted retargeting campaigns, refined SEO, and consistent follow-ups, we'll capitalise on all the interest generated in the previous quarters, converting it into tangible results.

Tracking and monitoring

In the final quarter, our main goal is to maximise bookings for 2025, so tracking bookings and return on investment (ROI) from paid campaigns becomes critical. We'll closely monitor the performance of early-bird offers and any countdown timers added to landing pages, paying attention to how many users are acting on these time-sensitive deals.

Tracking ad spend efficiency—how much we're spending on ads versus the number of conversions—is also essential in refining our strategy. At this stage, email click-through rates for time-limited deals and conversion rates for retargeting ads will reveal how effectively we're converting lingering leads.

Additionally, A/B testing for landing pages and ads can help us refine what messaging works best in driving last-minute bookings, ensuring we maximise our efforts before the end of the year. By continuously monitoring these metrics, we'll be able to tweak strategies in real time to achieve optimal results.

What if Mr & Mrs Egypt had day tours?

While Mr & Mrs Egypt currently specialises in multi-day tours, it's worth exploring how the strategy might shift if they moved into the day tour market. Day tours operate on a much tighter booking window, often attracting customers who make last-minute decisions once they've arrived at their destination.

To succeed in the day tour market, the marketing strategy must adapt to this faster decision-making process. The focus would shift toward search visibility, immediate engagement, and compelling calls to action that encourage same-day or next-day bookings.

The good news is that many of the strategies already recommended for multi-day tours can still be effective for day tours. A significant number of travellers research and shortlist activities before they arrive at a destination, but it's also crucial to capture the attention of those booking on impulse, with little prior knowledge of the brand. Here are some of the key adjustments that would be necessary:

First, the website would need to prioritise simplicity and speed. While the multi-day tour strategy focuses on creating a visually immersive experience, a day tour website needs to make fast bookings the priority. Customers should be able to reserve a spot within just a few clicks. Prominently featuring "Book Now" buttons, streamlining the checkout process, and displaying real-time availability are essential for converting last-minute bookings. Mobile optimization is critical, as many day-tour customers book on the go, meaning the mobile site must be intuitive, fast-loading, and easy to navigate.

SEO would also require a shift in focus. Keywords should be more location-based, reflecting the urgency of day-tour bookings. Terms like "day tours in Cairo," "last-minute Egypt tours," or "book a tour today in Luxor" should be prioritised to capture travellers looking for immediate experiences. Unlike the longer-tail keywords used for multi-day tours, these focus on customers who are already in Egypt or arriving soon and seeking quick, on-the-ground activities.

Content marketing would take a more direct approach. While the multi-day tour strategy leans on inspirational, long-form content, day tours require concise, action-oriented materials. Short blog posts or videos that provide quick insights like "Top Things to Do in a Day in Cairo" or "Best Day Tours to the Pyramids" would serve as digestible guides that drive urgency and immediate interest.

Email marketing would also shift from longer sequences to more frequent, short reminders about available tours, last-minute deals, and special promotions. Social media campaigns, while still valuing storytelling and engaging imagery, would focus more on urgency. Flash sales or limited-time offers like "Book a tour today and get $20 off" would cater to the spontaneous nature of day-tour bookings.

Local influencers and user-generated content could play a more prominent role as well. Collaborating with influencers actively in Egypt, sharing live experiences on platforms like Instagram Stories or Facebook Live, can help create a sense of immediacy and trust, further driving last-minute bookings.

Paid advertising should focus not only on geotargeting travellers already in Egypt but also on hyper-localised ads. For example, Facebook ads could target tourists at high-traffic locations like the Pyramids of Giza or Luxor Temple. These ads would place your brand directly in front of tourists looking for guided experiences at the exact moment they're making decisions about how to spend their day. Pairing this geotargeting with promotions like "Book today and save $20" or "Last-minute availability for today's tours" ensures you capture spontaneous bookings.

In conclusion, while many elements of the multi-day tour strategy can be repurposed for day tours, a more streamlined and immediate approach is necessary. The focus shifts to creating a sense of urgency, simplifying the booking process, and optimising for mobile. The key is balancing between those who plan ahead and those who make last-minute decisions, ensuring you capture both markets with fast, compelling content that converts.

Cancellation, experiencing and sharing

Now that we've established a comprehensive strategy for the earlier stages of the consumer journey—Dreaming, Planning, and Booking—it's time to shift our attention to the final phases: Cancellation, Experiencing, and Sharing. These stages are crucial for maintaining long-term relationships with customers, even after they've booked or, in some cases, cancelled.

By adopting the right tools and approaches, Mr & Mrs Egypt can transform every customer interaction—whether it's through cancellations, during the experience itself, or post-trip sharing—into an opportunity to build trust, inspire loyalty, and encourage future bookings.

Unlike the earlier phases, the strategies for Cancellation, Experiencing, and Sharing aren't tied to specific quarters. Instead, these are actions that should be woven into your business practises year-round, providing consistent value and maintaining ongoing customer engagement regardless of where your business stands in its marketing cycle.

Cancellation: navigating cancellations with a positive approach

While cancellations are inevitable in the tourism industry, they also provide an opportunity to create a positive experience that benefits your business in the long run.

Managing cancellations effectively can help you retain the trust and loyalty of your customers and possibly encourage them to rebook in the future. Here's how to integrate a cancellation strategy into the overall 12-month marketing plan for Mr & Mrs Egypt.

Show empathy in your communication

Cancellations can offer valuable insight into your customers' needs or the challenges they face. It's important to approach each cancellation with empathy, as the reasons behind a cancellation can vary significantly. Perhaps the customer's travel plans changed, or they might be dealing with a serious family matter. You can't know for sure, so it's essential to communicate with understanding and support. This approach leaves the door open for future bookings, even if their initial plans didn't go through.

Email strategies

Cancellation acknowledgment: Send an immediate, personalised email when a cancellation occurs. Thank the customer for considering Mr & Mrs Egypt, express understanding, and offer a gentle reminder that they're welcome to rebook whenever they're ready.

For example: *"We understand that plans can change, and we're sorry you won't be joining us for this trip. If you ever wish to rebook in the future, we'd love to welcome you to Egypt. We hope everything is well with you, and we look forward to seeing you soon."*

Post-Cancellation Survey: 24 hours after a cancellation, send a follow-up email politely asking for feedback on why they cancelled. This will help improve your service and identify areas for future growth.

For example: *"We'd love to understand how we can improve. If you have a moment, please let us know why you had to cancel. Your feedback helps us enhance the experience for all future guests."*

Re-Engagement Email: After a month or so, send a friendly reminder of Mr & Mrs Egypt's offerings, possibly with a special offer.

For example: *"We'd love to welcome you back when the time is right! As a thank-you for considering us, we're offering a USD$200 discount on your next booking. We hope to see you in Egypt soon."*

Phone your customer

Since Mr & Mrs Egypt provides high-value products, consider making a personal phone call after a cancellation. This allows for a more empathetic, direct approach and gives the customer an opportunity to reschedule.

For example: *"Hi [Customer Name], this is Carol from Mr & Mrs*

Egypt. We noticed you had to cancel your trip, and I just wanted to check in personally. Is everything alright? Is there anything we can do to assist you?"

If appropriate, mention an upcoming exclusive tour or offer a rebooking discount during the call.

Build trust with flexibility

Offering flexibility is a key way to build customer trust. Make your cancellation policy clear, simple, and flexible. Highlight this across all marketing channels—on the website, in booking emails, and on social media—to reassure potential customers that they won't be penalised for unforeseen circumstances.

Offer trip protection plans

Providing travel insurance or trip protection during the booking process can help reduce anxiety and encourage bookings. Partner with an insurance provider or develop an in-house protection plan to offer customers peace of mind, and promote it prominently during the booking stage.

As an added bonus, you can skim a commission off the top if your customer takes out insurance!

Turning cancellers into advocates

Even when a booking is cancelled, you can still turn the situation around by offering exceptional customer service. Encourage customers who had to cancel to leave a review about their positive

experience with your service, showing future customers that Mr
& Mrs Egypt handles every situation with care.

Tracking and analytics for cancellations

Track cancellation rates, reasons for cancellations, rebooking rates
post-cancellation, and customer satisfaction after a cancellation.
These metrics will help refine your sales and marketing strategies,
your payment policies, and provide valuable insights into customer
behaviour.

Experiencing: delivering a share-worthy experience

The experiencing stage is where Mr & Mrs Egypt's guests are finally
on the ground, enjoying everything the company has to offer. This
is a pivotal moment in the customer journey—one that can solidify
brand loyalty or, if not handled well, lead to disappointment.

Marketing also does not stop now that they are in-destination. In
the experiencing stage, the marketing focus should shift towards
enhancing the guest experience in real-time, fostering emotional
connections, and providing opportunities for them to share their
journey. Not only does this stage create lasting impressions, but it
also sets the stage for positive reviews and repeat business. Here
are some ideas to consider...

Welcome communication

Send a warm, personalised welcome email or SMS the day they

arrive in Egypt. This small gesture reassures them that Mr & Mrs Egypt is ready to deliver an outstanding experience. This message should include a reminder of their itinerary, emergency contact numbers, and a friendly note to set the tone for their trip.

Real-time support

Offer easy-to-access customer support, whether through WhatsApp, SMS, or live chat, so guests can easily get assistance if they encounter any issues during their trip. This helps maintain their confidence and keeps the experience stress-free.

Surprises and delights

Consider adding unexpected small touches to enhance the experience—complimentary drinks during a Nile cruise, a photo book from their trip, or even a handwritten thank-you note from their guide. These little moments of joy turn a great experience into a memorable one that people are more likely to share.

Encouraging real-time sharing

The experiencing stage presents a great opportunity for user-generated content (UGC). Encouraging customers to share their adventures as they happen not only promotes your brand in real-time but also helps you reach a broader audience through authentic, real-time testimonials.

Create a branded hashtag, such as #MyEgyptJourney or #ExploreWithMrAndMrsEgypt, and actively encourage customers to use it when sharing their photos and stories on social media. This is a simple yet effective way to gather UGC and spread brand awareness. You can incentivise this by offering small rewards, like a small gift during the tour.

Photo opportunities

Provide opportunities for guests to take share-worthy photos by including picturesque stops in your tours. Let them know that you're happy to snap photos for them or point out the best spots for an Instagram-worthy shot.

Branded souvenirs

Create small, branded souvenirs or keepsakes that customers can take home. These can be given as part of the tour or offered at a small additional cost (better if free!). A thoughtful keepsake not only reminds them of the experience but also reinforces your brand.

Sharing: turning customers into brand advocates

This phase is all about converting satisfied customers into vocal advocates for your brand. Whether through social media posts, reviews, word-of-mouth recommendations, or testimonials, the sharing stage plays a critical role in expanding your brand's reach. When handled correctly, this stage can significantly boost credibility, attract new customers, and reinforce loyalty among existing ones.

In the sharing stage, your goal is to encourage and facilitate customer-generated content and feedback, turning their personal experiences into valuable marketing assets.

Follow-up email requesting review

After the trip, send a personalised email thanking them for choosing Mr & Mrs Egypt, along with a clear call to action to leave a review on Google or a platform like TripAdvisor (where possible, use Google!). Be sure to include direct links to these platforms to make the process as easy as possible for the customer.

Feature customer stories

One of the most impactful ways to build trust and inspire future travellers is by showcasing standout user-generated content (UGC) on your social media channels and website. Featuring real customers and their stories adds a layer of authenticity that resonates strongly with potential travellers.

Consider creating a dedicated 'Customer Stories' section on your website. This area could showcase testimonials, travel diaries, and photos from past guests, offering visitors a genuine glimpse into the experiences of others who have travelled with Mr & Mrs Egypt.

A great example of this approach is the 'Guest Stories in France' section we helped develop for France of a Lifetime. Since their tours are entirely custom, and have no bookable tours online, we created this area to serve as a living case study.

The stories are told from the customer's perspective, highlighting how France of a Lifetime delivered exceptional service and unforgettable experiences. Each story includes photos and even short video reviews, where customers share their personal journeys and how the company made it all possible.

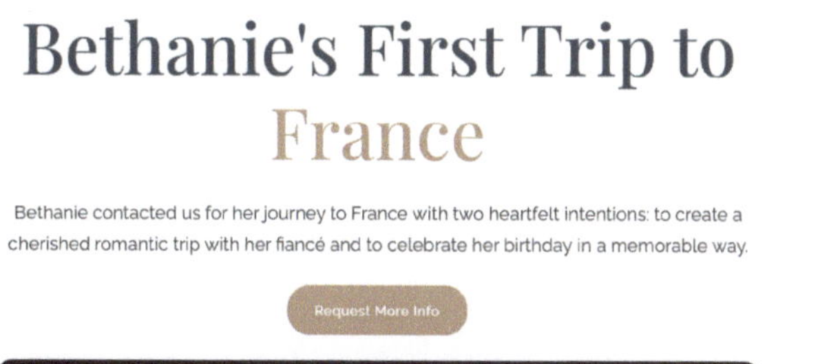

This type of page accomplishes two things: First, it allows potential customers to envision themselves in those experiences, planting the seed of desire to become the next featured guest. Second, it showcases the company's exceptional service, making the decision to book a tour seem like a no-brainer.

Mr & Mrs Egypt should implement a similar strategy to harness the power of their satisfied customers' experiences, turning them into a valuable marketing tool that builds trust and inspires future bookings.

Photo contests

Host a photo contest that encourages customers to share their best photos from the trip. Offer a prize, such as a discount on a future tour for them or a friend, or a travel gift, to the winner. This not only generates buzz but also provides you with a library of high-quality photos you can use in future marketing efforts.

Referral program

Launch a referral program where past customers can earn rewards for referring friends or family. Offer a discount or special perk for both the referrer and the new customer. For example, a customer who refers a friend could receive USD£200 off their next tour, while the friend receives the same welcome discount on their first booking.

Final thoughts

With the entire 12-month strategy now laid out, we've covered everything from capturing the imagination of the potential customers in the Dreaming stage to nurturing them through the Planning and Booking phases, and even how to maintain those vital relationships through Cancellations, the Experiencing stage, and into the Sharing phase. The goal throughout this journey is not just to make a sale, but to build lasting, meaningful connections with your customers—connections that turn first-time bookers into lifelong advocates for Mr & Mrs Egypt.

While this strategy offers a clear roadmap for building and maintaining a successful brand, Carol and Atef may not be able, or willing, to implement every suggestion. It's also important to remember that marketing is a fluid, ever-evolving process. The strategies outlined here provide a solid foundation, but adapting to feedback, staying on top of market trends, and continuously refining your approach are essential for long-term success.

 For those eager to dive even deeper, the download section of this book offers additional resources, including a more detailed breakdown of the strategy, worksheets, and a comprehensive visual guide that maps the entire customer journey. This will help you understand how each element fits together, ensuring that you can implement the plan effectively and see the results for yourself.

Ad strategy secrets: reaching your ideal audience every time

Before diving into the results for Mr & Mrs Egypt's strategy, I want to share some highly effective online advertising techniques you should consider for your own campaigns.

When it comes to running ads, it's not just about reaching the most people—it's about reaching the right people, at the right time, with the right message.

Too many businesses throw money at ads and hope something sticks, but that's a costly gamble. Instead, I'm going to reveal some ad targeting secrets that can significantly improve the effectiveness of your campaigns, helping you guide potential customers from dreaming about their next trip to finally booking it. Always remember, every aspect of marketing should align with the three stages of the customer journey: Dreaming, Planning, and Booking.

Introducing the Omnipresent Ad Strategy

An Omnipresent Ad Strategy works across the different stages of the customer journey—Dreaming, Planning, and Booking. This is the exact approach we used for Mr & Mrs Egypt, ensuring a consistent presence in front of potential customers at each step of their decision-making process.

The core of the Omnipresent Ad Strategy is to guide the customer smoothly along their journey, from initial inspiration all the way to booking. This strategy allows you to stay in front of the target audience with a series of tailored ads that inspire, build trust, and encourage action. It's designed to run in the background for months, without constant updates, working seamlessly to capture the attention of travellers when they're ready to make decisions.

For Mr & Mrs Egypt, we began by targeting affluent travellers in key markets like the US, using detailed demographic filters. Our awareness ads focused on inspiring content, such as how to plan a trip to Egypt and what unique experiences await beyond the pyramids. These initial ads engaged those in the Dreaming stage by sparking their curiosity and showcasing Egypt as a rich cultural destination.

As potential customers moved into the Planning stage, retargeting ads offered more specific, personalised content. These ads introduced Carol and Atef, the faces behind the brand, through videos that built trust and demonstrated expertise. The messaging reassured travellers about safety and the ease of planning a custom tour.

By the time users reached the Booking stage, the ads were more direct, driving users to book a consultation or inquire about specific tour packages. These ads featured clear calls to action, customer testimonials, and compelling offers to convert lookers into bookers.

Building an Omnipresent Strategy

An omnipresent ad strategy ensures your audience sees a consistent stream of relevant ads throughout their journey. The secret is retargeting. Rather than bombarding everyone with the same ad, you use tailored ads based on where the customer is in their journey. For most campaigns, I use a structure consisting of one or two main ads targeting a specific customer persona, then 12 retargeting ads, broken down into four subsections.

Main targeting ads

These ads introduce your brand to new audiences, casting a wide net to attract those in the Dreaming stage. For Mr & Mrs Egypt, we targeted potential customers in the US, aged 40-65+, with interests in Egypt, archaeology, and related topics. We also refined our audience based on household income brackets, ensuring we reached those with the financial means to book luxury tours.

Our main ads focused on delivering value, such as "How to Plan a Seven-Day Trip to Egypt," inviting travellers to start dreaming. These ads led to a landing page full of itineraries and calls to action, like scheduling a consultation or exploring tour options.

After testing, we found that the seven-day planning ad outperformed a downloadable PDF guide we also initially offered— so we scrapped the PDF ad. Testing and optimisation are crucial in any campaign. The budget for these main ads was £20 per day.

Retargeting ads:

Retargeting ads are where the magic of the omnipresent strategy happens. This is how you stay in front of potential customers as they progress through the dreaming, planning, and booking stages. For Mr & Mrs Egypt, we created 12 retargeting ads, each costing only £1 per day, categorised as follows:

1. Value ads (dreaming stage)

The first set of three ads focuses on providing value and inspiration to the audience. At this stage, potential customers are still in the Dreaming phase, considering Egypt as a destination but not yet planning their trip. These ads highlight Egypt's unique experiences and aim to spark curiosity, enticing them to explore more.

- **How to Choose the Best Nile Cruise in Egypt:** This ad directs users to a blog post, providing practical advice on selecting the right cruise. It's an ideal piece of content for those just beginning to imagine their trip.
- **A Guide to the Best Restaurants in Egypt:** Another value-driven blog post, this ad targets food lovers, offering insight into Egypt's culinary delights.
- **6 Awesome Places in Cairo That Most Visitors Don't See:** This ad highlights hidden gems in Cairo, drawing attention to the lesser-known attractions that make Egypt more than just a visit to the pyramids.

By repurposing existing content, these ads create a low-effort, high-impact way to engage users early in their travel journey.

2. Expertise ads (transitioning to planning)

As users move closer to the Planning stage, the next set of ads focuses on demonstrating the expertise of Mr & Mrs Egypt. This is the stage where trust is built, and the brand starts positioning itself as the ideal guide for their Egyptian adventure.

- **Meet Carol and Atef:** A video ad introducing the faces behind the brand, showing their deep knowledge of Egypt's culture and history. This ad is designed to build a personal connection, giving potential customers confidence in who they'll be working with.
- **Beyond the Pyramids:** A video showcasing Egypt's broader range of experiences beyond the iconic pyramids. It's an essential piece to educate potential customers on why Egypt is a more diverse destination than they might realise.
- **Is Egypt Safe for Female Travellers?:** Addressing a common concern for female travellers, this ad builds trust by directly answering safety questions, further reinforcing the brand as a reliable and considerate guide.

These ads aim to strengthen the relationship by providing expertise, answering common questions, and making the customer feel more comfortable as they begin to plan their trip.

3. Social proof ads (further into planning)

As users become more engaged with the brand, it's crucial to provide social proof to push them closer to booking. These next three ads focus on customer testimonials and reviews, demonstrating that others have had positive experiences with Mr & Mrs Egypt.

- **Customer Testimonials:** A series of ads highlighting past client reviews, building trust by showcasing real experiences. These testimonials give users the reassurance they need to continue their planning process.
- **Visual Testimonials:** Though Mr & Mrs Egypt did not have

video reviews at the time, image-based testimonials were used effectively. If available, video testimonials would be even more impactful.

- **Trip Reviews with Star Ratings:** Simple, image-based ads featuring 5-star ratings and direct quotes from satisfied customers, designed to build credibility and encourage further engagement.

These ads help reinforce the brand's reputation, making potential customers feel confident about choosing them for their trip.

4. Call to action ads (booking stage)

Finally, the last three ads focus on driving conversions. These are the most direct ads, targeting users who have shown strong engagement with the brand and are ready to take action.

- **Book a Consultation with Us:** A video ad featuring Carol, inviting potential customers to schedule a consultation. This ad leads to a landing page where users can either book a call or fill out a contact form.
- **Write Your Own Adventure:** An image carousel ad encouraging users to customise their own Egyptian itinerary, linking directly to a form on Facebook to make the process as simple as possible.
- **18-Day Egypt Luxury Experience:** An alternative option for users not interested in custom tours. This ad promotes a pre-planned, 18-day luxury tour, guiding users to a specific landing page with all the details.

Ongoing retargeting and google display ads

In addition to the Facebook ads, Google Display Ads are layered into the strategy, keeping the brand in front of potential customers who may have visited the site but didn't take immediate action. These ads appear across the web, gently nudging users back to the Mr & Mrs Egypt website, reminding them of the offers and encouraging them to continue their journey through the booking funnel.

By using a combination of omnipresent ads on Facebook and Google Display Ads, we're able to create multiple touchpoints with potential customers. It's often said that a customer needs to interact with a brand around seven times before making a purchasing decision, and this strategy ensures those touchpoints are meaningful and consistent throughout the customer journey.

Why this strategy works

The power of the omnipresent ad strategy lies in its ability to follow potential customers at each stage of their journey. It's not about aggressively pushing sales—it's about offering a steady stream of useful, inspiring content that builds trust, engagement, and ultimately, bookings. Whether someone is daydreaming about their next trip, actively planning, or ready to book, your ads are there, providing value and nudging them in the right direction.

One of the biggest mistakes businesses make is failing to deliver the right message at the right time. The omnipresent strategy ensures that each touchpoint—whether it's inspiring someone with a dream-worthy destination, showcasing your expertise, or encouraging them to take action—feels timely and relevant. You're not just advertising; you're guiding your audience through their entire journey, keeping your brand front and centre.

This level of precision targeting not only maximises your ad spend but also increases your chance of converting potential customers by reaching them where they are.

How an Omnipresent Strategy works for day tours

Adapting the omnipresent strategy for day tours requires a slightly different approach, given the more immediate nature of these experiences. While multi-day tours often involve long planning cycles, day tours tend to attract travellers who are already in-destination or making last-minute decisions. The key here is to create ads that emphasise urgency and convenience while still maintaining the storytelling and value-based framework of the omnipresent strategy.

For day tours, retargeting ads can focus on messaging that drives immediate action, such as "Book Now and Start Your Adventure Today!" or "Limited Spots Available for Tomorrow's Tour." This sense of urgency taps into the spontaneity of day-trippers, encouraging them to seize the opportunity before it's too late.

Since many of these customers are already in your destination, using geotargeting to serve ads based on their current location is crucial. Ads can be shown to tourists near popular landmarks, hotels, or even airports, making it easy for them to discover and book a nearby experience on short notice.

It's also important to remember that not all day tour bookings happen on a whim. In fact, many travellers start researching and shortlisting activities well before they even arrive at their destination. This is why outbound marketing remains an essential part of the omnipresent strategy for day tour operators.

Some travellers, especially those with limited time, plan their activities in advance to ensure they make the most of their trip. They'll often search for unique, must-do experiences and compare options long before they board their flight. By targeting these travellers early you can position your day tour as a must-book experience, ensuring it's already on their shortlist by the time they arrive.

In this context, the omnipresent strategy ensures that your tours remain top-of-mind for those planning ahead, while also enabling you to retarget them when they're closer to booking or after they've arrived. The balance here is key: combining in-destination marketing with outbound strategies that reach travellers in the dreaming and planning stages, so your day tours become the obvious choice when they're ready to book.

 You can download the Omnipresent overview diagram for Mr & Mrs Egypt in the download area.

Geotargeting: reaching travellers where they are

One unique strategy I recommend is geotargeting high-traffic tourist areas. For example, you can target ads around iconic landmarks such as the Pyramids of Giza, the Statue of Liberty, or Edinburgh Castle. Additionally, consider placing ads near major airports or in areas with a high concentration of hotels, where tourists are likely to stay. This also allows you to personalise your ads.

Localised ads

Say you are running ads over Edinburgh Castle, make mention of the fact they are there. As an example, you run food tours in Edinburgh, then your ads could state;

'Hungry after climbing all those steps at Edinburgh Castle? Then come and meet us outside for some traditional 'Scran' (Scottish for food), drink and banter. (Scottish for good chat). We have tours that depart every two hours so book now and meet us right outside the castle!'.

See what I mean? You can have some real fun with these ads.

Targeting cruise ships

If your destination caters to cruise ship passengers, Facebook's location-based ad tools can also be incredibly effective. You could target ads at passengers as they dock at ports, offering exclusive tours and experiences for those who might have only booked basic shore excursions through their cruise line. You could even show ads along specific cruise routes, ensuring your brand stays top of mind before they disembark.

AirBNB targeting

As mentioned before, another powerful tool AirDNA. This platform provides insights into short-term rental trends, occupancy rates, and seasonal demand in specific locations. By analysing AirDNA data, you can identify clusters of rental properties where tourists are staying and target ads to those areas.

This way, you're increasing the likelihood that your ads are seen by people actively staying in your destination, further enhancing your chances of capturing their interest.

Section five
The results

**So, how did our strategy perform 18 months on?
The short answer: very well.**

Although we initially developed a 12-month strategy, I'll be covering an 18-month period to account for the crucial early phase, which focuses heavily on building the brand.

While we didn't get to implement everything exactly as planned—such as the podcast idea—almost all of the other elements were launched, albeit with a few tweaks to some of the content topics. As expected with any long-term strategy, we had to make adjustments along the way, adapting to feedback and market shifts. What matters is that the core strategy was executed, and we saw some significant progress.

Carol and her team also took charge of social media management, as I firmly believe that no one can handle it better than the people who live and breathe the business every day. The tour guides, storytellers, and those directly involved bring an authentic voice that simply can't be replicated. With our guidance and expertise to back them up, they can connect with their audience in a way that feels genuine and truly reflects the spirit of the company.

I'm going to break down the results into three 6 month periods, starting from the launch of the new website. This will give you a clear view of how the plan unfolded and the impact it had over the course of this period. As you'll see, we had a few wins, faced a couple of challenges, and uncovered opportunities for ongoing refinement—because, as we've learned, a marketing strategy is always evolving. Let's dive in...

First six months: building the foundation

Brand awareness, SEO and rankings

When Mr & Mrs Egypt launched their website, the SEO performance over the first few months was promising, especially for a brand-new site in such a competitive travel market. This phase was about laying the groundwork—establishing a presence, attracting the right traffic, and building awareness.

Traffic started strong, with 1,370 sessions in the first full month. As often happens with new websites, there was a slight dip in traffic in the second month, followed by a 27% rebound in October, bringing the total sessions for the quarter to 3,133. These fluctuations were expected as the site refined its content and engagement strategies.

Notably, about 78% of the traffic came from new visitors—a great sign for a growing brand. However, keeping these visitors engaged was an initial challenge. Bounce rates ranged from 77% to 85%, and session durations were under a minute, suggesting room for improvement in user engagement.

At this early stage, social media was the primary traffic driver, contributing 74-80% of visits, with organic search accounting for just 13%. However, we already began to see encouraging signs of growth in organic search, with a 34% increase in sessions in October compared to the previous month. Key terms like "Egypt luxury private tours" also saw significant ranking improvements, which set the stage for future growth.

Gaining momentum: SEO, ads, and organic traffic growth

Organic search evolution

As we moved into the second phase of the SEO journey, the strategy began to take hold, and organic traffic showed steady growth. High-value keywords like "Egypt luxury tour packages" and "Egypt historical tours" started driving more targeted, high-quality traffic, confirming that the site was gaining traction in competitive search rankings.

Session durations improved as well, reflecting deeper engagement with the content. However, we knew that more work was needed to further engage visitors and move them closer to booking. To achieve this, we expanded the site's content, adding more in-depth travel guides and visually rich pages that better showcased the unique experiences Egypt had to offer.

Paid ads: supporting organic growth

During this phase, we also launched a series of Facebook and Instagram awareness ads targeted at affluent travellers in the US and UK. These ads aimed to support our organic efforts, particularly during the Dreaming stage of the customer journey, and focused on promoting custom tours.

Our ads were designed to inspire curiosity, with titles like "How to Choose the Best Nile Cruise in Egypt" and video ads like "Beyond the Pyramids." Retargeting ads then kicked in, guiding users who interacted with these earlier ads toward the Planning stage by showcasing testimonials and demonstrating expertise.

Targeted engagement: retargeting and social proof

Retargeting and personalised content

As the campaign progressed, retargeting ads became a critical component. Once visitors were familiar with the brand, we used more personalised content to build trust and demonstrate the unique expertise of Carol and Atef. The "Meet Carol and Atef" video ad was particularly effective, driving users to a landing page with clear calls to action—either scheduling a consultation or filling out a contact form.

We also addressed common concerns, such as safety for female travellers, through targeted ads like "Is Egypt Safe?"—allowing us to speak directly to high-intent audiences and offer reassurance.

Social proof and testimonials

We reinforced trust by leveraging customer testimonials in our ads. Although video reviews were not available at the time, we created visually appealing image ads featuring real customer feedback. These ads were highly effective in building credibility and pushing users from the Planning stage into Booking.

Conversions and final push: booking stage ads

In the final stage, we shifted towards direct calls to action, targeting users who had already visited the site or interacted with previous ads. The "Book a Consultation with Us" video ad, featuring Carol, was instrumental in driving final conversions, leading potential customers to the custom tour page.

We also introduced additional ads, such as "Write Your Own Adventure" for custom tours and "Book an 18-Day Egypt Luxury Experience" to appeal to those interested in longer, pre-planned tours. These ads directed visitors to booking pages, providing clear paths for them to make their reservations.

Results from the ad campaign

The paid ad campaigns were incredibly successful. Over 30 days, the campaigns generated 50 qualified leads, representing 70 individual travellers. These leads had a potential sales value of between £190,000 and £910,000, depending on the tour packages booked. With a total ad spend of around £1,400, the return on investment was impressive. Even with a modest 10% conversion rate, Mr & Mrs Egypt stood to generate between £19,000 and £91,000 from these leads—a clear indication that the strategy was working.

Measuring success: traffic sources, engagement, and conversions

Diversification of traffic sources

By the end of the campaign, one of the major successes was the diversification of traffic sources. Organic search became the primary driver of traffic, contributing nearly 70% of total visits compared to 42.91% at the start. This growth was a direct result of our ongoing SEO efforts, combined with the support of the paid ads.

Social media, direct traffic, and referral traffic also continued to play significant roles in driving visitors, reducing reliance on any single channel and creating a more stable, diversified traffic flow.

Engagement metrics and conversion growth

The engagement rate saw a significant jump, with visitors spending more time on the site, reflected by the increase in session duration from 1 minute 51 seconds to 2 minutes 27 seconds. More importantly, inquiries and bookings increased steadily as the user journey was streamlined and made more engaging.

Conclusion: a strategy that delivered

As the campaign progressed, Mr & Mrs Egypt continued to see strong results. Over the 18-month period, they secured 131 bookings, generating a total revenue of £434,262. These figures reflect not only the effectiveness of the targeting and engagement strategies we implemented but also the growing brand recognition and trust built through consistent marketing efforts.

Importantly, during this time, Mr & Mrs Egypt accumulated a substantial number of customer reviews. This played a critical role in reinforcing the trust-building element of their brand. As positive reviews grew on platforms like TripAdvisor, they provided invaluable social proof, encouraging potential customers to trust and book with confidence. These reviews became a key component of the overall marketing strategy, helping to convert leads who were further along in the decision-making process.

Overall, these results highlight how a well-executed marketing strategy can turn interest into bookings and deliver significant revenue, even for a relatively new business in a competitive market. With clear objectives, carefully crafted messaging, and a multi-layered approach, Mr & Mrs Egypt was able to grow from initial brand awareness to tangible, long-term success.

Challenges and resilience

Despite the campaign's success, Mr & Mrs Egypt faced a significant challenge towards the end of the 18-month period—the impact of the war in Gaza, which borders Egypt. At the early stages of the conflict, many travellers became cautious, resulting in a number of cancellations. This understandably affected the business's overall performance during this time, and without these unforeseen cancellations, the results could have been even stronger.

However, the groundwork laid through consistent marketing and brand-building proved invaluable during this period of uncertainty. The focus on showcasing the unique experience of Egypt, alongside messaging that emphasised safety when travelling with trusted experts like Mr & Mrs Egypt, became critical. The efforts to position the company as a reputable, reliable brand helped them regain traction even amidst the difficult geo-political situation.

The 18 months of strategic marketing not only created a solid foundation for the business but also helped it weather this challenging period. The trust built through customer testimonials, transparent communication, and the expert guidance provided by Carol and Atef reassured potential clients. As a result, despite the initial wave of cancellations, Mr & Mrs Egypt was able to maintain stability and continue attracting bookings.

The marketing strategy for Mr & Mrs Egypt delivered substantial results, driving growth and securing significant revenue even in the face of external challenges. The brand's reputation and resilience, fostered through ongoing marketing efforts, have positioned them for continued success moving forward.

Final word from Carol

It seems only fitting to give the last word to Carol, who has been on this incredible journey from the very beginning. Her story captures the essence of what it takes to build a successful tour company—passion, persistence, and the right guidance.

Here's Carol, in her own words, reflecting on her experience:

I first came across Chris Torres when I had the idea to create a tour in Egypt based on Agatha Christie's Death on the Nile. As I was researching how to turn this idea into reality, I stumbled upon Chris' podcast, The Digital Tourism Show. The podcast was a goldmine of ideas and inspiration, so I decided to look up Chris's company, TMA.

At the time, the concept was still just a vague idea in my head, so it wasn't the right moment to engage a marketing agency. But I did read the first edition of Lookers Into Bookers cover to cover, and it gave me plenty of valuable advice and ideas to try.

Then COVID hit, and I lost my job. While this was a difficult time, it gave me the space to truly think about what I wanted to do with the tour. As fate would have it, Chris was offering a special deal to help support tour companies through the pandemic—it was an opportunity too good to pass up. That's when we launched Literary Tours in Egypt, with our flagship tour, of course, based on Death on the Nile. Chris and TMA were instrumental in getting everything off the ground. I already had the name, but Chris created the logo, website, and a full marketing plan for us.

This initial success led my husband, Atef, and I to resurrect his tour business, which had been left dormant since the revolution in Egypt in 2011. We were essentially starting from scratch. The website was outdated, the brand name didn't reflect what we did, and we had no marketing strategy in place. The entire tourism industry had changed in the years since the revolution, and Atef felt that his knowledge was out of date, while I didn't have much experience in the industry at all.

It was clear to us that we needed help, so we turned to Chris once again. We started with market research, which was fascinating and helped us clarify our goals. From there, we fully engaged Chris to help us revive the company. The process also brought to light something surprising—what I thought we wanted to do and what Atef thought we wanted to do were quite different! Fortunately, Chris and his team guided us through every step, and we felt we were in safe hands.

The day Chris revealed his ideas for our brand was one of the most exciting moments of this journey. I was absolutely blown away by how well he understood who we are and what we stand for.

He captured it all perfectly in the brand name and logo—Mr & Mrs Egypt was born. The logo, featuring two Egyptian cats, was nothing short of perfect. Atef and I were both speechless, and I even burst into tears. To this day, I love our brand. It truly represents us, and it's something that resonates with our customers, too. In fact, many of our reviews on TripAdvisor refer to us as Mr Egypt and Mrs Egypt! We never could have come up with this ourselves.

From there, the hard work began—building the website and creating our core tours. While we were involved every step of the way, Chris and his team did the heavy lifting. Whenever I had some outlandish idea (which happened quite often), Chris and his team gently steered me back to our core principles and messages.

We launched the brand, and while success wasn't immediate due to the pandemic, we steadily built a following. Word of mouth played a big part in our growth, and the consistent message of Mr & Mrs Egypt appealed to our target audience. Atef, with his incredible local connections, and me, with my understanding of what visitors to Egypt really want, made for the perfect partnership.

The brand that Chris created didn't just reflect who we were; it also helped guide our business decisions. Mr & Mrs Egypt became one of the greatest achievements of my life, and I'm proud to say that despite the challenges we've faced, we're still here, offering high-quality, custom-made tours of Egypt. Our glowing reviews on TripAdvisor show that we're still delivering on our vision, and the brand continues to be at the heart of that success. We simply wouldn't be where we are today without Chris.

While we were fortunate to afford Chris's marketing services, I know that's not an option for everyone. That's why this new edition of Lookers Into Bookers is so valuable. It's packed with Chris's knowledge, experience, and insights, and I'm honoured that Mr & Mrs Egypt is featured in it. Whether you're just starting out or looking for fresh ideas for your existing business, this book is full of practical advice and inspiration. I wish every reader the same success we've had with Mr & Mrs Egypt.

Join the community... and other resources

While I hope you found this book extremely helpful, I advise that you continue the conversation through the following communities and resources.

Tourpreneur

tourpreneur.com

Joining the free Tourpreneur community is an invaluable step for any tour operator or travel business owner looking to stay ahead in this dynamic industry. By becoming part of this community, you'll connect with like-minded professionals, share insights, and access a wealth of practical knowledge from experts who understand the challenges and opportunities within tourism.

Whether you're seeking advice on growing your business, optimising your marketing strategies, or navigating industry trends, the Tourpreneur community offers ongoing support and resources tailored to your unique needs. Joining the community means you won't be alone on your journey; you'll have access to a thriving network ready to help you succeed.

Tourism Marketing Agency

tourismmarketing.agency

If you're looking for help to grow your tour or activity business and boost direct bookings, partnering with my agency, the Tourism Marketing Agency (TMA), is a game-changer.

Specialising in tourism marketing, we understand the unique

challenges of the industry and offer tailor-made solutions to help you stand out in a competitive market. From crafting effective marketing strategies to managing paid ad campaigns, my expert team is here to guide you every step of the way.

Whether you're a small business looking to scale or need help with SEO, paid advertising, websites or email marketing, TMA is dedicated to helping you increase bookings and reduce reliance on OTAs.. turning lookers into bookers.

The Marketing Coach

themarketing.coach

If you're a business owner with an internal marketing team but are seeking expert external advice and guidance, The Marketing Coach is designed specifically for you. My coaching services offer tailored support to help you and your team navigate the complexities of tourism marketing, from refining your strategy to optimising digital campaigns.

With personalised coaching sessions, I provide actionable insights that complement your existing efforts, ensuring your team has the tools and knowledge they need to drive results.

Whether you're looking to fine-tune your approach or scale your business, I'll work alongside you to unlock your full marketing potential, giving you the confidence to achieve your goals.

Software and tools mentioned in this book and others I recommend

Sitemap Generator .... https://www.xml-sitemaps.com
Screaming Frog .... https://www.screamingfrog.co.uk
Hotjar .... https://hotjar.com
Crazy Egg .... https://www.crazyegg.com
SEMrush .... https://www.semrush.com
GTMetrix .... https://gtmetrix.com
BuzzSumo .... https://buzzsumo.com
SpyFu .... https://www.spyfu.com
ThemeForest .... https://themeforest.net
Social Pilot .... https://www.socialpilot.co
Social Blade .... https://socialblade.com
Calendly .... https://calendly.com
Descript .... https://www.descript.com
Monday.com .... https://www.xml-sitemaps.com
MailerLite .... https://www.mailerlite.com
TipDirect .... https://tripadmit.com

About Chris Torres

Chris is an author, podcaster, and an expert in brand development and digital marketing for tourism, boasting an illustrious 34-year journey in the industry. He speaks at global tourism events where he shares his knowledge and insights, guiding how travel, tourism, and destinations can catapult their brand recognition and boost bookings.

At the helm of the Tourism Marketing Agency, Chris has honed a niche in tour operator marketing, attracting a clientele that spans continents, with over 90% based outside the UK, including some of the industry's largest operators.

Author of the best-selling marketing book, "How to Turn Your Online Lookers Into Bookers", Chris encapsulates practical marketing tactics across 400 pages dedicated to the tours and activities sector, making the elusive art of online conversion an attainable feat for many.

Beyond the pages, Chris manages a thriving community of over 14,000 operators under the banner of Tourpreneur. Through workshops, podcasts, and an engaging Facebook Group, Chris and his partners orchestrate a platform of continuous learning, sharing, and growing, embodying the spirit of communal success.

www.ingramcontent.com/pod-product-compliance
Lightning Source LLC
Chambersburg PA
CBHW041233050726
47599CB00007B/942